A DESCRIPTIVE HISTORY

OF THE

IRISH

CITIZEN ARMY

D1344113

Kevin Morley

3/2186564

© 2013 Kevin Morley

The front cover image is the statue of James Connolly
opposite Liberty Hall, Dublin Ireland.
The back cover image is the statue of Jim Larkin,
O'Connell Street Ireland
Photography by Sofian Murphy

All rights reserved. No part of this publication may be reproduced
in any form or by any means—graphic, electronic or mechanical,
including photocopying, recording, taping or information storage and
retrieval systems—without the prior written permission of the author.

ISBNs
Parent 978-1-78237-149-6
Epub 978-1-908817-59-4
Mobi 978-1-908817-60-0

A cip catalogue for this book is available from the National Library.

Published by Original Writing ▮▮▮▮▮n, 2013.
Printed and B▮▮▮▮▮▮▮▮▮▮▮▮▮▮▮▮▮▮▮▮vorldwide.com

This work is dedicated to my parents

Olive and Nick Morley

Preface

This short work is, as far as possible based on the information available, a description of one of the more obscure elements contained in Irelands revolutionary past, the Irish Citizen Army. It is not the intention to go into the rights or wrongs of the army, the reader must do that, though whether I have been successful or not is for the reader to decide.

To collate information I have used witness statements courtesy of the Army History Bureau National Archives Dublin (hereafter referred to as The National Archives), as the only available primary source. Secondary sources used are older works on the subject, particularly the writings of Frank Robbins (Irish Citizen Army) and without either source nothing would have been possible. Information on the Irish Citizen Army is not easy to ascertain therefore what is available had to be maximised.

Contents

INTRODUCTION

Not a great deal has been written in the annals of Irish history regarding the Irish Citizen Army, mainly because there does not appear to be a large amount of information available. Both the National Museum and the Labour History Museum on enquiry to both establishments had little if anything to offer. However the National Archives did have *"Witness Statements"* from volunteers of the Irish Citizen Army which have been used during the course of this work. It is possible that this shortage of usable information could have something to do with the fact that the Irish Citizen Army was almost exclusively working class and its aims were the promotion of the interests of the wealth creators, the proletariat of Ireland. With Ireland now being a modern bourgeois state and upholder of the capitalist free market system there appears to be a reluctance even by modern labour institutions to acknowledge the revolutionary role played by the working class in the independence movement. We must also remember that at the time of the Dublin Lockout and formation of the Citizen Army, 1913, the Employers Federation was led by William Martin Murphy, a nationalist MP and supporter of Home Rule, though not a republican and only, it would appear, for the Irish capitalist class, a man who could in one respect be described as a modern variant of Henry Grattan, who in his day advocated the vote for all Catholics and Protestants above a certain class status. This piece of work is an attempt by a socialist from England to try and redress that imbalance in Irish history which has been less than fair to the Citizen Army, the armed wing of organised labour.

The Irish Citizen Army is often reported to have been a tiny force, which, in terms of weaponry it was having only sufficient armoury to equip around two hundred personnel. On closer examination according to the late T.A, Jackson, in his work *Ireland Her Own*, 'if it could have got the arms, it could have paraded ten times that number'. Many people who may have joined the Citizen Army joined, instead, the Irish Volunteers because of the availability of weapons which that organisation afforded them. The Irish Citizen Army was born out of the events which took place during the lockout of 1913 and was based almost exclusively in the Dublin and immediate area, unlike the Volunteers whose membership covered a greater geographical terrain.

The veteran dynamiter, Thomas Clarke of the Irish Volunteers, once heaped praise on the Citizen Army regarding their training and discipline, which he attributed to the fact that they were led by three former British soldiers, James Connolly, Michael Mallin and Richard McCormack. These three men were ex British servicemen who had joined the forces of the crown for economic, and economic reasons only and not at the time for weaponry training, though this would prove an asset in latter years.

Perhaps the most accomplished work to date on the citizen army would be R.M. Fox's book *'The History of the Irish Citizen Army'* which I have used for a number of references, though there are chapters in other more modern works which are well worthy of reference. Chapter 36 in *James Larkin Lion of the Fold* by Donal Nevin et al and chapter31 in *James Connolly A Full Life* again by Donal Nevin are worthy of the readers attention. It is probably very important for the reader to grasp the initial role of the Citizen Army at the beginning of its inception in 1913 as a workers defence force, a force which was greatly needed as locked out men and women were getting seriously injured by the drunken attacks of the DMP (Dublin Metropolitan Police) and RIC (Royal Irish Constabulary) resulting in the tragic deaths of two men during such a confrontation, with officers under the influence of alcohol, James Nolan and James Byrne both dying from the injuries received by beatings from policemen's truncheons. Another man, ironically also called James Byrne, from Dun Laoghaire who was the district organiser of the Irish

Transport and General Workers Union died after going on hunger and thirst strike in protest against being jailed on trumped up charges resulting from his involvement in the Lockout. The Irish Citizen Army slowly became moulded into a revolutionary Red Army, predating Trotsky's much larger variant in revolutionary Russia, which took a lead role in the Easter Rising.

A theme constant to this work around the time of the 1916 Easter Rising are Connolly's inner and outer thoughts regarding the Irish Volunteers. There were public expressions of solidarity and implicit trust coupled with private reservations concerning the Irish Citizen Army's relationship with the Volunteers. Certainly for the duration of Easter week the two organisations fought as one even though James Connolly privately held niggling doubts as to the political depth of the Volunteers. It is not the intention to over labour this point but it is a very important issue, and one which had echoes well after Connolly's death. During the War of Independence the sounding vibes of orations made by Connolly prior to Easter week still bore relevance. I have given my own opinion as to what Connolly was saying in both his private and public declarations regarding relations and compatibility with the Volunteers but the reader must, however, come to their own conclusion as I, like most others speak from an opinionated point of view not necessarily held by all. We can only draw conclusions based on the written evidence available all of which are the valued opinions of others, and my opinion is no exception to this rule. As James Connolly, or anybody closely associated with him, is no longer available for comment on the matter, and further documentation appears unavailable, we shall perhaps never know exactly what his position was on this subject.

After the 1916 rising the history of the Irish Citizen Army becomes somewhat obscure. However this does not mean that it went out of existence. After the execution of James Connolly James O'Neil assumed command. The Irish Citizen Army, as a body, took no major part in the war of independence, 1919-21, though individuals and groups from the organisation did, and although keeping their autonomous identity, as Citizen Army members, fell under the overall command of Oscar Traynor, OC republican forces in Dublin. It is, however, reasonably acknowledged that the last time this body of men and women marched as a force was at Jim Larkin's funeral in 1947. However this does not mean that the tradition of the Irish Citizen Army in modern Ireland has gone because there are organisations in the republican and socialist movements today which would claim to be the inheritors of the same Irish Citizen Army. The movement most striking to myself would be the "Irish Republican Socialist Movement" particularly its armed wing the "Irish National Liberation Army". In its 2007 Easter publication of *Starry Plough* it states on page 11 'James Connolly was a leader in the Easter Rebellion and a Socialist Revolutionary, a mammoth voice in the labour movement and defender of working people. He opposed the free state, he opposed partition, he opposed home rule, he opposed Imperialism, Capitalism and their wars and he was demonised as a terrorist also. He led a small armed force, the Irish Citizen Army, who ideologically were the predecessors of the INLA, with no ideological difference what-so-ever, against the British Government and it was against the will of the majority of the time (sic). The majority did not support the Rebellion and, in fact some, even fought against it. It's just like today and its all down to ignorance coupled with the effectiveness of Imperialist/Capitalist propaganda'. It is up to the reader to make up their own mind on the authors opinion on this matter, as it is only an opinion and is based on written information available.

The flag most associated with the Irish Citizen Army was the Starry Plough, or the Plough and the Stars which it has been claimed initially consisted of a green background with a yellow/gold plough and seven points of the plough depicted by the equivalent number of stars, and was designed, it is broadly thought, by a man named Megahy. However Sean O'Casey, Hon. Secretary to the Citizen Army, in the early days, states

4

that the first design of the flag had a blue background which disappointed the volunteers of the Irish Citizen Army because it was **not** green. The modern variant of this flag consists of a blue background with seven white stars arranged in the same formation. Initially, it is thought the flag was to represent the Irish rural workforce, Ireland been very much a rural country at the time. However with the outset of the 1913 Dublin lockout it took on a more industrial meaning and is today a representation of both the industrial and rural working class and is claimed by a number of organisations including occasionally the Irish labour party. Research into the '*Starry Plough*' flag proved to be laborious with only one piece of credible work available that being a book on *Irish Flags* by G.A. Hayes McCoy which was available for use in the Reading Library, Pearse Street Dublin and which I have used.

It is hoped by the author that this piece of work will enlighten those who are interested in the Irish Republican and Socialist tradition and give a clearer understanding of that tradition and those who claim to be the modern inheritors of the said same tradition. This assumption by these organisations, and it is not the purpose of this work to say whether their claims are justified or not, is a matter for the reader to dissect. It is not the role of the author to argue for or against any organisations claim to be the inheritors of the Irish Citizen Army tradition. The purpose of the book is not to dictate peoples opinions but, hopefully, give a clearer understanding of one factor in the history of the Irish labour and republican traditions.

1

THE EARLY DAYS

Most people who are involved or take an interest in Irish Labour History, and/or Irish Republican historical bodies will have some knowledge of the Irish Citizen Army. The initial role, at its inception during November 1913, of the Irish Citizen Army was that of a workers defence force to counter the bosses hired thugs of the DMP (Dublin Metropolitan Police) and RIC (Royal Irish Constabulary) and their excessive measures of violence on behalf of the employers resulting on one infamous occasion in the deaths of two men, James Byrne and James Nolan both dying of their injuries received because of police brutality. These were the results of disturbances which occurred on Saturday 30th August 1913 'hundreds of people, including thirty policemen, were injured and required medical attention in the hospitals. Two civilians died from their injuries: James Nolan, who died in the early hours of Sunday from the effects of a fractured skull, and James Byrne, who died subsequently from injuries received in one of the baton charges' (*James Larkin Lion of the Fold*: Donal Nevin et al. P 180). Another man from Dun Laoghaire, also named James Byrne and unfortunately until November 2007 has been forgotten died after undertaking a hunger and thirst strike against his imprisonment on trumped up charges which resulted in his release from Mountjoy Gaol after one week. However unfortunately for Byrne days after his release he died from pneumonia in Monkstown hospital almost certainly as a result of the damage his body suffered during his week long strike. At the funeral of James Byrne of Dun Laoghaire the oration delivered by James Connolly said: "The police vultures and master vultures were not content until they had got Byrne into prison. He had been thrown into a cold, damp, mouldy cell, but while in prison, so contemptuous had he been of those who put him there that he refused food and drink. If their murdered comrade could send them a message it would be to go on with the fight for the sacred cause of liberty, even if it brought them hunger, misery, eviction and even death itself, as it had done Byrne" (Source *Dun Laoghaire Express*, 9th November, 2007).

To some the finest hour of the Irish Citizen Army may well be the heroic role, alongside the Irish Volunteers, undertook during the course of Easter week 1916. To others, without demeaning those events, the part played by the Irish Citizen Army and its leadership in bringing discipline, proletarian discipline, during the long and arduous months of the 1913 Dublin Lockout to the ranks of the Irish working class would be of equal importance. My own belief is that both complemented each other. Perhaps in the Post Modern world of industrial relations and public demonstrations where it is not uncommon for protestors to have their skulls caved in by the forces of law and order it could be argued the Citizen Army, or its equivalent, is badly needed.

The formation of the Irish Citizen Army through to its fruition, though not full potential, could be described as a staggered process. On 12th November 1913 a meeting of the Industrial Peace Committee took place in the rooms of the Reverend R.M. Gwynn at 40 Trinity College. Here the idea of a workers defence force was discussed, having been ruled out of order at a previous meeting, and arrangements were made 'for a drilling scheme for the locked out workers and a fund opened to buy boots and staves, with Professor David Houston of the Royal College of Science as treasurer' (*James Connolly A Full Life*: Donal Nevin: P.553). If this idea formulated by the Industrial Peace Committee, which also included Captain J. White a former British army officer, had stopped at its initial intention of bringing discipline into the ranks of the locked out workers and defending pickets from the excesses of the police then it is perhaps unlikely that it would have ever developed any further than this. It is, in all probability, realistic to say that when the lockout came to an end in 1914 then so too would the embryonic Citizen Army. Had the more progressive and, indeed, aggressive persons not taken this idea of the committee and moved it forward then it is highly unlikely that this body would have taken part in the Easter Rising of 1916. The chances of it developing into anything more radical and/or revolutionary were remote simply because those, with the possible exception of Captain White who held romantic notions and dreams as opposed to concrete plans, were formulating the initial idea for the formation of this force were not revolutionary. The main, and perhaps only reason of their initiative was to instil some discipline into the locked out men and to give them some defence against the excesses of the DMP and RIC while at the same time combating evictions and the wanton destruction of their tiny dwellings. The last thing the Rev. Gwynn and the rest of the Industrial Peace Committee had in mind was a radical workers militia which would develop into a revolutionary socialist army, which is precisely what happened.

As has briefly been explained the initial role of the Irish Citizen Army was one of a workers defence force. Perhaps the incidents of "Bloody Sunday" and the resulting deaths of Byrne and Nolan gave extra impetus to the need for some kind of defence force. However even if the Citizen Army had been in existence at the time of these incidents it is perhaps unlikely they could have done a great deal to prevent the unfortunate deaths. Equally unlikely is the notion they could have prevented "Bloody Sunday" simply because the forces of the state were overwhelmingly superior in equipment and manpower. This should not be taken as a deficiency on the part of the not yet formed Irish Citizen Army, because we will never know what they could or could not have done at the time but the reason, in my opinion, that little could have been done is because the organisation was stretched and lacked resources, though certainly not courage, and it was to take almost three more years to develop into a force of any real significance. The Citizen Army was at the time of the lockout a new ideological force which was inexperienced and poorly armed and it is a credit to the men and women involved that the theory was ever put into practice at all.

* * *

Big Jim Larkin was a very charismatic and militant trade union leader and organiser was a formidable enemy of any employer. He will go down in the annals of labour history, not only in Ireland and Britain but across Europe and the United States along with parts of the former Soviet Union. His speeches and actions will share the company of such people as his first Lieutenant during the 1913 Dublin Lockout, James Connolly, along with such people as A.J. Cook (Secretary of the Miners Federation of Great Britain during the 1926 General Strike) and in more recent times Arthur Scargill (President of the National Union of Mineworkers during the year long 1984-85 miners strike) as well as people in the United States such as big Bill Haywood, Joe Hill and Elizabeth Gurley Flynn of the Industrial Workers of the World.

From the outset of the Dublin Lockout in August 1913 the whole weight of the capitalist class and their agents were aimed against Larkin, Connolly and the Irish Transport and General Workers Union (ITGWU). The pro-unionist *Irish Times* newspaper, which was the chief rival of the *Irish Independent*, owned by W.M. Murphy the employers knight in white armour during the lockout, echoed its rival by writing on 3rd September 1913: 'The employers of the City of Dublin have at last made up their minds to free themselves from an intolerable tyranny. The strike organisers are at bay . The struggle may be sharp, but we do not think it will be a very long one, and the result will more than justify whatever of money or peace the city may have to pay for it. Within the last few days Messrs. Jacob and other large firms have refused to deal with members of the Irish Transport Union. Yesterday the Dublin Coal Merchants Association came to a similar decision. They gave reasons for which must satisfy every fair minded man' (*In The Footsteps of Big Jim: A Family Biography*: Jim Larkin Jnr.P.56). By "every fair minded man" the

9

newspaper was obviously referring to the employers and those who supported the bosses and by "the city" the *Irish Times* and other pro capitalist newspapers, the overwhelming majority, meant the business fraternity and not the working class which constituted the larger part of the population and whose poverty and misery the bourgeois media could care nothing.

The unions own publication fought back the best it could on far more meagre resources than their capitalist counterparts. On Saturday 13th September, 1913, *The Irish Worker* wrote a letter of support for Jim Larkin for his so called unlawful address delivered from the balcony of the Imperial Hotel on Sunday 31st August to the locked out workers. Larkin was disguised as an elderly gentleman and was dressed in Casmir Markievicz's (husband of Constance) frock coat.

> *'Dear Jim*
> *Your performance at the Imperial Hotel on Sunday last was magnificent and not likely to be forgotten; but your impersonation of William Martin Murphy as president of the meeting of the meeting of the Chamber of Commerce, on the following day will surely live in history.*
> *Your denunciation of Larkin and Larkinism was fine; it could not have been better done by Murphy himself'.*

The letter was signed

'Yours admiringly Red Hand', *The Irish Worker* Saturday September 6th 1913. For full text of the letter read P.58-59 *In The Footsteps of Big Jim*. The first few lines of the letter were an obvious reference to Jim Larkin caricaturing W.M. Murphy, hence the disguise as an eloquent elderly gentleman which served more than just an outfit to gain entry to the hotel. The incident at the Imperial Hotel resulted in police baton charging the crowd causing untold injuries, that day August 31st 1913 will always be known certainly in trade union and labour circles and perhaps beyond, as Bloody Sunday.

Larkin made many rousing speeches both in Ireland and Britain during the lockout. One such message stated 'men be men! The fight goes well we are winning, and shall smash Murphy and his Federation of tyrants to smithereens if you keep straight on'(Larkin jnr. P.60). Such sentiments were regular features of Jim Larkin's "fiery cross" speeches.

Big Jim also had enemies within the broader trade union, labour and nationalist movements. We should not forget that William Martin Murphy, owner of the Dublin United Tramways Company where the lockout began and proprietor of the *Irish Independent* newspaper was also a nationalist MP and moderate supporter of Home Rule. Arthur Griffith completed the united nationalist front of anti-Larkinism by denouncing Larkin unreservedly in the name of *Sinn Fein*, he was also to condemn the Easter Rising three years later in the name of the same organisation. It should also be remembered that the same Arthur Griffith was no republican, he supported a dual monarchist situation similar to that of Austria and Hungary of the time. There was also much reaction against Larkin and Connolly within the ranks of the labour movement, where there appeared several newsletter with anti-Larkin and ITGWU propaganda. The newsletter which is of most interest to us in this section was called the *Toiler* which was a little paper or newsletter cramped with densely tight written columns presented on very cheap paper. The editor of this publication was a renegade socialist called P.J. McIntyre whose principle subject appeared to be a hatred of Jim Larkin, whom he had first locked horns with back in 1909. He was a former Dublin branch secretary of the British based union the "Workers Union" and he had once toyed with the idea of bringing the membership of this union in Ireland into Larkin's Irish Transport and General Workers Union. However McIntyre's reasons for this merger were largely based on economic gain and self interest resulting in when this veil had been lifted and a deal with Larkin failed to materialise he, McIntyre, embarked on a campaign against English strike mongers and supporters of Larkin (Larkin received considerable support from rank and file trade unionists in Britain. A fete which was to be reversed some seventy years later during the miners strike in Britain 1984/85). This campaign was supported by the nationalist head of *Sinn Fein*, Arthur Griffith (the policies of Sinn Fein at that time should not be compared or confused with the policies of either of the modern *Sinn Fein* parties). Griffith, it must be made clear, was not a republican but a nationalist. He advocated a dual monarchy strategy with an Irish Parliament under the British Crown, which is often referred to as the Hungarian Way with reference to the Hungarian Parliament of the day under the Austrian Kaiser. Griffith published and supported many of McIntyre's anti strike articles in his journal the *United Irishman*.

McIntyre's parting of the ways with Jim Larkin led to the former being expelled from the Independent Labour Party after which he spent much of his time denouncing socialism, syndicalism and various forms of anarchism, the I can't have my own way so I'll stamp my feet syndrome. By 1913 P.J. McIntyre , now also sacked from the Workers Union for pursuing an anti-Larkin policy which led him down the evil vindictive path of strike breaking, a policy which in trade union circles is tantamount to treason, against the ITGWU. McIntyre, through the pages of the *Toiler*, began launching the most extraordinary allegations against Jim Larkin. One such bizarre fantasy was that he, Larkin, was the son of an informer named James Carney. Carney was the man who betrayed the breakaway Fenian group the Invincibles who had executed the Viceroy Lord Frederick Cavendish and his permanent Under Secretary Thomas Henry Burke in the Phoenix Park on May 6th 1882. 'McIntyre's evidence was Larkin's striking resemblance to ....members of the.... Carney family and the fact that Larkin, like Carney, had shown himself to be an able organiser of the most reckless elements in the Irish Capital. McIntyre challenged his enemy to prove him wrong. Larkin at first ignored the baiting, but the *Toiler* persisted. It even went as far as to publish photographs in December of a bearded Carney and of Larkin sporting the false beard he was wearing when arrested on Bloody Sunday, asking readers to tell the difference' (*Lockout Dublin 1913* Padraig Yeats: P404). The aim of these ridiculous allegations prosecuted by McIntyre was to totally discredit Larkin firstly by challenging him to prove the place and birth of his parents. The problem faced by big Jim, and McIntyre knew it, was that he could not produce a birth certificate for his parents, which was not unusual for the time. For the record Jim Larkin's father, James senior, was born in Armagh, 1849, and his mother Mary McAnulty was born in Liverpool 1842. Big Jim himself was born in Co. Down and not, as many to this day sincerely believe, in Liverpool where he was perhaps registered. Unfortunately Jim Larkin could not produce the relevant birth certificate therefore, so McIntyre's argument went, the theory he put forward that Larkin was the son of the informer James Carney could not be disproved. However very few people apart from the right wing nationalists and employers, who perhaps didn't believe it either but their purpose was served by pretending to, and the renegade socialists would believe such folly.

These then were some of the lengths which the unholy alliance of the nationalist right wing, including Griffith and people masquerading as socialists like P.J. McIntyre would go to discredit big Jim Larkin. A similar parallel could be drawn between McIntyre and, in more recent times, a man named Roy Lynk who helped form and led a breakaway pro-establishment union, the Union of Democratic Mineworkers, during the 1984-85 miners strike. This union was funded by Thatcherite right wingers within the higher echelons of big business and was part of an orchestrated campaign to discredit the National Union of Mineworkers President, Arthur Scargill. The UDM failed, as it was supposed to once it had served its purpose to save one single coalmine and Lynk goes down in the lower echelons of class collaborator and traitor.

Against this backdrop big Jim Larkin and others including Captain Jack White and Constance Markievicz were to set about organising the Irish Citizen Army.

* * *

When the idea of a Citizen Army was suggested to Jim Larkin, who was in prison at the time, he was enthusiastic, as was his deputy James Connolly. The thoughts of Jim Larkin turned to the events which were taking place in Ulster since the signing of the 1912 covenant pledging resistance to Home Rule by around 500,000 people. Here a Dublin lawyer called Edward Carson (prosecutor in the trial of Oscar Wilde) had been campaigning against Home Rule in any shape or form and had whipped up opposition to the point bordering on hysteria. The number of signatures he obtained is sizable enough but under the circumstances prevailing in those parts at the time not that difficult. The employers were threatening anybody who did not sign with unfortunate "consequences". Therefore even for a person with Sir Edwards narrow bigoted philosophy half a million signatures would not have been excessively difficult, and from this anarchy the Ulster Volunteer Force was born. Larkin looked on the formation of the UVF as a form of inspiration, for totally opposite reasons, towards the formation of a radical workers militia which was to become known as the Irish Citizen Army. Larkin argued that if it was good for the likes of Carson and the Ulster Volunteers to arm and drill then it was just as good for the working men of Dublin to do the same. As can be seen Jim Larkin had developed the initial idea of the Industrial Peace Committee a couple of stages further along the road in the development of the Citizen Army which would peak in revolutionary armed struggle.

Jim Larkin's, some would say hijacking, of the Industrial Peace Committees idea and developing and radicalising it further was shared by James Connolly who was, perhaps even more farsighted. Connolly had an even more advanced role in mind for the Citizen Army in so far as to what it would eventually become. He looked further and deeper than Larkin's perception as to what was taking place in Ulster. He was looking further a field and back in time to the events which took place following the defeat of France in the Franco Prussian war 1870-71. In Paris there was formed a commune based on workers and soldiers control of society in a democratic way. The Paris Commune, as it has become known, gave birth to what many describe as the first ever Red Army in Europe. Former enemies, the French and Prussian bourgeoisie, crushed the commune ruthlessly forgetting their past differences in favour of class solidarity against the greatest threat to bourgeois rule of them all, the working class. The revolutionary forces of the commune fought back bravely against the most advanced armies in Europe of the time and gave inspiration to those future generations who wished to fight back against the repressive capitalist status quo.

Connolly also visited events even further away, though slightly more recent, in Moscow 1905. The Moscow insurrection was to bear many similarities to the events which were to take place in Dublin eleven years later, the Easter Rising. The conditions of the workers and peasants in and around Moscow had reached an all time low and the time for a fight back against Tsarist autocratic rule had come. Connolly wrote of the background to the Moscow insurrection: "In the year 1905, the fires of revolution were burning very brightly in Russia. Starting with a parade of unarmed men and women to the palace of the Tsar, the flames of insurrection spread all over the land. The peaceful parades were met by volleys of shrapnel and rifle fire, charged by mounted Cossacks and cut down remorselessly by cavalry of the line, and in answer to this attack, general strikes broke out all over Russia. From strikes the people proceeded to revolutionary uprisings, soldiers revolted and joined the people in some cases, and in others the sailors of the Navy seized the ironclads of the Tsars fleet and hoisted revolutionary colours. One incident in this outburst was the attempted revolution in Moscow". The events which took place in 1905 could well be described as the precursor to the even more momentous events which would occur in October/November (depending on which calendar is used) 1917 Russia, the Russian Revolution.

Connolly studied these events and, as perhaps only he could, perceived the possibilities along the revolutionary road towards socialism for the Irish Citizen Army. With Captain White using his military knowledge in organising drilling and discipline coupled with the correct political leadership the possibilities were without bounds. Connolly himself had a military training from his days as a British soldier in the Kings Own Liverpool Regiment. He was also studying the street fighting techniques adopted by the aforementioned revolutionary forces of Paris and Moscow. James Connolly was farsighted and imaginative enough to see the possibilities embodied in the idea of a workers defence force but also realistic enough to realize these were still early days in the development of the Irish Citizen Army.

The Irish Citizen Army went through three stages in its development. The basic idea as discussed by the Industrial Peace Committee as simply a workers defence corps was then developed by Jim Larkin into something more radical. This development stage was given inspiration by the antics of Edward Carson and the UVF in the North of Ireland and irrigated Larkin's belief that what was good for the reactionary forces in Ulster was equally applicable to the progressive ideas held by the working men of Dublin. Jim Larkin's development of the initial idea was an important contributor in paving the way for Connolly's fruition stage.

By fruition it is not meant to imply that the Irish Citizen Army reached its full potential development because the conditions prevailing at the time prevented this from being achieved. For example had the 1913-14 Dublin Lockout ended with a more favourable result for the proletariat, or had the outcome of the Easter Rising been kinder to the Irish then perhaps this full potential may have been recognised. What is meant by fruition is it reached the most advanced stage of development as a revolutionary force which the conditions of the time would allow. That revolutionary pinnacle was to be the events of Easter week 1916.

***

The workers gathered outside Liberty Hall one evening late in 1913 awaiting the appearance of their leader Jim Larkin and his lieutenants to deliver their address. The faces of these same workers 'turned with concentrated uneasy patience towards the window on the left hand side of Liberty Hall, waiting for it to be raised, that they might listen to their nightly message of hope, progress and encouragement from those same leaders, whom they were convinced would guide them through the heavy ordeal that each man must share that there might be preserved for all the elemental right of the workers to choose their union' (*James Larkin Lion Of The Fold,* Donal Nevin ed. P.253). The right of working people to join a union of their own choosing was one of the fundamental principles which led to the long Winter months known as "the Dublin Lockout" of 1913-14. Out of this lockout was to emerge arguably the first Red Army in Europe, arguably because the events of the Paris Commune 1870-71 obviously pre-dated its formation as did the episodes in Moscow during 1905 as has been mentioned. However the Irish Citizen Army can certainly lay claim to be the first Red Army of the 20th century in Western Europe which pre-dated Leon Trotsky's organisation in revolutionary Russia, Eastern Europe, by four years.

Larkin was more than a little aware that the workers of Dublin were in the battle of their lives against the titans of capital. The employers had joined forces under the umbrella of the "Employers Federation" (precursor of the modern IBEC) which consisted of 400 employers against workers represented by 37 unions, and Larkin, along with James Connolly, knew this was a battle for survival, a class war for their lives. "Therefore the workers must become disciplined, organised, made of one stuff in thought and action". These were the words of Jim Larkin as he addressed his audience. He continued 'They must no longer be content to assemble in hopeless, haphazard crowds, in which a man does not know and can not trust the man that stands next to him, but in all their future assemblies they must be so organised that there must be a special place for every man, and a particular duty for each man to do' (Nevin ed. 254). These were some of the embryonic words which were to lead, on that same evening, to the popularisation of the ideas which would form the Irish Citizen Army. As Jim Larkin continued his address 'Labour in its own defence must begin to train itself to act with disciplined courage and with organised and concentrated force. How could they accomplish this? By taking a leaf out of Carson' (Nevin ed P. 255). What was good for Carson and his Unionist cohorts in the North of the country to organise against Home Rule and the aspirations of the Irish people then it was equally correct for the forces of labour to organise against the aggressive capitalist class and their allies, native or foreign through a Citizen Army.

Larkin then announced to his audience that they were to be given a military training, that is those who wanted one which was by far the majority if not unanimous, and the man to instruct them in this training was Captain Jack White. There was a feeling of immense optimism amongst the crowd as loud cheers rang out to this announcement, the mood was that such a move was perhaps long overdue and a tone of ecstasy descended over the masses. Labours achievements and possibilities would know no boundaries 'with an army trained and disciplined by officers who held the affection and confidence of the workers' (ibid). Captain White stated that the "Irish Citizen Army would fight for labour and for Ireland". He asked "all those who intended to second their efforts by joining the army and training themselves for the fight for social liberty, to hold up their hands". He was not to be disappointed as almost in unison the hands were held aloft against the darkening sky accompanied by a loud deafening cheer which proclaimed the birth of the Irish Citizen Army on the evening of November 13th 1913. The military wing of organised labour, with more than a touch of revolutionary syndicalism about it, came into being. To briefly clarify the last point, syndicalism is a form of revolutionary trade unionism advocating the overthrow of capitalism and the seizure of economic and political power through one big union, OBU, using industrial muscle and the general strike. Both Jim Larkin and James Connolly advocated this form of trade unionism, especially the sympathetic strike, as one way of ultimately bringing about the demise of the capitalist system, therefore ending the exploitation of labour by capital.

As was mentioned above the Irish Citizen Army was perhaps unique in the labour movement becoming the first Red Army in Western Europe, although their aim was perhaps not yet revolution. William Martin Murphy, leader of the Employers Federation during the Lockout, claimed in a statement to a Royal Commission of Inquiry into the events of Easter week that 'Captain White had discussed the idea with him and had pointed out that when the strikers were drilled they would be disciplined and it would raise their moral tone. Larkin and Connolly, however had other ideas for the new force' (Nevin 258). However not too much credence should be given to this reported conversation because a) Murphy was renowned for his conservatism with the truth especially when it involved the Transport Union and the Lockout and, b) some of whites writings for the *Irish Worker* had more than a hint of revolution about them. For example he wrote before the end of 1913: "Whether the fruits of your labour is the freeing of yourselves or the freeing of your country, time will show. But ultimately Ireland can not be free without you nor you without Ireland. Strengthen your hand then for the double task". These kind of statements would hardly compliment Murphy's interpretation of the said statement. How serious Connolly took White as a potential revolutionary is open to question but on one occasion he, White, remonstrated with Connolly about his army being taken off to a political meeting without notification been given. Connolly responded by saying "you're nothing but a great boy" and

Nora Connolly recalls White once in a terrible rage, "his hands clenched and fairly gnashing his teeth at some misinterpretation of a command he had given" and her father remonstrating with him, "easy now Captain, remember, they're volunteers". However despite the early differences between Connolly and White the Irish Citizen Army was no longer an embryo but a living being embodied by comradeship and common cause. This comradeship became even more apparent, even to the casual observer, once Connolly had assumed command after Larkin's departure for the United States. A noticeable feature even in the early days of James Connolly's stewardship was the unswerving loyalty held by the volunteers towards the man and his socialist ideology and direction much of which was based on the writings of Karl Marx. Connolly the uncompromising socialist had the rare gift of being able to reflect his ideas to such an extent that they were mirrored by the rank and file of the army. Connolly's total commitment to gender equality was plain to all but those afflicted with the highest level of ignorance to see. Although the race and ethnic question did not exist, at least to any major degree, in those days of the early twentieth century it should be seriously assumed, based on Connolly's internationalist theories of comradeship, that Connolly would have extended those same principles of equality to all such minorities. Perhaps a thought some of those would be modern disciples of James Connolly should seriously think about.

Although in these early days weaponry and uniforms were virtually non existent the enthusiasm within the ranks more than compensated for this shortfall. The Aungier Street branch of the ITGWU had formed a band with instruments which were paid for by the men on hire purchase. 'They had annoyed the police by playing the "Peeler and the Goat" and the police threatened to smash their instruments. The workers promptly formed a guard for their band armed with Hurley sticks and the idea of a workers defence force soon caught on' (*A History of the Irish Working Class*: P. Berresford Ellis, P.201). The first drilling sessions took place using Hurley sticks in place of rifles, and these same hurlies were carried on route marches, and would carry a kick to match any policeman's truncheon. On the part of the volunteers of the Citizen Army there was no lack of enthusiasm to use these hurlies as an antidote to the batons of the DMP and RIC. weaponry and uniforms would eventually be acquired.

3/2186564

2
THE PLOUGH AND THE
STARS (STARRY PLOUGH)
THE FLAG OF THE IRISH CITIZEN
ARMY

As the fledgling Irish Citizen Army developed into an organisation which could be identified with the name "army" it became a point of major consideration that it, the army, should have a flag, or colours as the term would be known in military circles. The flag was to be unique among the flags of Ireland, and was specific to the Irish Citizen Army, unlike the Gold harp on a Green background which was claimed by various organisations including, among others, the Ancient Order of Hibernians an organisation which was an antithesis to organised labour and socialism. The same Gold Harp on Green background was flown by the Citizen Army over its Citadel, Liberty Hall, before the Easter Rising but the Plough and the Stars was to be a specific emblem to the army of organised labour. It was also to differ from the `republican tricolour of Orange White and Green which was modeled very much on the flag of revolutionary France, Red, White and Blue (combining the old Royal White with the Red and Blue colours of Paris) , and was indeed brought to Ireland by Thomas Francis Meagher and put together by daughters of 1798 exiles and descendants of the Wild Geese. It was brought back from France in 1848 by Meagher and was first exhibited at Waterford and later at a public meeting in Dublin where it was received with much enthusiasm. The tricolour however was a national emblem and covered all classes representing both the Orange and Green traditions separated by the White of peace and the nation including the

capitalist class. The Plough and the Stars however was to be the flag of the working class and was not to be interpreted in any other way.

It is by no means certain who first came up with the idea that the Citizen Army should have its own colours but according to information traceable back to Sean O'Casey, playwright and secretary of the Irish Citizen Army in the early days, the original suggestion of a flag or emblem came from Jim Larkin, secretary of the ITGWU and Commandant of the Citizen Army. The flag, as previously mentioned, was to be of a design completely 'different from any Irish flag previously known' (*History of Irish Flags*: G. A. Hayes McCoy P.215). The Plough and the Stars, Starry Plough, was to make its first appearance on the 5th April 1914 at an Irish Citizen Army meeting. 'Of a unique and beautiful design it shows a stylised representation of an agricultural plough with, superimposed upon it, a representation of the constellation Ursa Major, the Great Bear or Plough of the heavens- all on a green field bordered by a gilt fringe' (ibid).

The original design, as opposed to the practical presentation, was as described but on a blue background. A drawing of this design was presented to the National Museum of Ireland in Dublin, now located at Collins Barracks, in 1954. It is not known definitively as to the reason behind the changing of the background colour, from blue to green, as was represented on the original design occurred but there is one theory, which has credibility, and that is the volunteers of the Citizen Army were less than pleased with the blue background and had a strong preference for the green of Ireland. Credit for the original design of the flag is generally attributed to the Belfast artist of the time William H. Megahy who was working as an art lecturer in the School of Art located in Kildare Street, Dublin. Although the plough did not precisely represent the tool of the urban proletariat, so to speak, it did constitute a method of production in rural labour. At the time it must be taken into account that Ireland, outside Dublin and Belfast, was a rural country with agriculture as the main source of production and subsistence. The ITGWU, parent of the Irish Citizen Army, were organised within the agricultural sector and therefore the Plough would have been an appropriate symbol of rural working class struggle and toil. The Dublin during the period under present discussion bore little identity with the City we know today, for example, in 1913 Ballymun was an agricultural village therefore the design of the flag needed to be representative pertaining to the working environment at the time.

'The symbolism of the design is most appropriate, most eloquent. Here is the workers dream come true. He has beaten the sword which represents his struggle - and represents his bitter memories of the 1913 strike- if not into the Ploughshare of Isaiah into what is certainly the more harmonious part of his design, the coulter' (Hayes McCoy P, 216).

As has already been mentioned the Plough itself can not be strictly regarded as the instrument of labour used by the Dublin proletariat of the period but is, never the less an instrument representing the toil of working class people across the nation. It may be worthy of mention at this point that because in 1954 an ageing Sean O'Casey in order to reconcile his by now dimming memory 'of a blue flag with the green flag now in the National Museum suggested that there might have been two Irish Citizen Army flags-the blue one which he remembered and the green one flown on the Imperial Hotel, the latter's very amateur attempt to copy the original flag' (Hayes McCoy 216-17). O'Casey argued at the time that "Connolly might have had the original colour changed to green because he (Connolly) was a nationalist, as well as a supporter of syndicalism (revolutionary form of trade unionism advocating a general strike as the starting point for overthrowing capitalism in pursuit of socialism) , at heart and liked the colour, as witness his hoisting the green flag on Liberty Hall on Palm Sunday". This could be another attempt by Sean O'Casey to undermine the socialism and internationalism, nationalism generally though not exclusively an antithesis to internationalism, of James Connolly because he, O'Casey, hated the idea of the Citizen Army taking part in the Easter Rising at all. Connolly saw the national liberation of a nation, a nation consisting of the working class and proletarian control of the means of production, as an inherent component part of internationalism and socialism, national liberation can only be achieved in its full sense with socialism at its core. It is of little use without socialism as the working class will still be under the yolk of a native capitalist dominance resulting in exploitation of that class by an indigenous bourgeois strata whose soul aim is to maximise profits at the expense of the working class. 'O'Casey had already said in 1919 that the Palm Sunday flag was a tricolour! Memory is as fickle as a changeful dream' (ibid), or memories can be altered to suit the prejudices and wishes of the individual. Perhaps Sean O'Casey's memory was geared to convince the listener what the orator wanted them to believe, who knows but it is broadly accepted that the poet rarely missed an opportunity to undermine Connolly in latter days.

To this day there is still some dispute over who designed the flag in the first place despite William Megahy taking most of the credit with, yet again, what may be described as a confused O'Casey claiming another candidate for the grand pattern claiming 'the one who actually designed it is disputed, some saying AE-George Russell, the poet and essayist- but went on to say that when he, O'Casey, asked Russell he denied the honour' (Hayes McCoy: P. 216). The playwright had another theory as to the origins of the flag and that was it could have been made by the "Dun Emer" Guild. As Sean O'Casey's legacies are for the best part the only information available, even accepting that in later life his memory may have been distorted, we have to go on in ascertaining the origins of the colours of the Irish Citizen Army it is this data we must base our conclusions. This may well be one of those questions which will never be adequately answered, though I firmly believe on the evidence available William Megahy should be credited (opinionated view), and as time passes the origins and designer will become increasingly vague. Sean O'Casey said much on the subject but, as has been mentioned, he had developed many differences of opinion with the Irish Citizen Army and in particular James Connolly. Therefore some of his interpretations and recollections may have been be a little loaded to suit his own position. Whatever or whoever brought about the Plough and the Stars, Starry Plough, there is no disputing that this emblem of organised labour flew triumphantly over the Imperial Hotel, O'Connell Street (Sackville Street at the time), owned by arch capitalist William Martin Murphy during Easter week.

In 1934 an attempt was made to reconstruct the Flag of the Irish Citizen Army and as a result of these efforts an entirely new version, with no doubt the same meaning, evolved. It should be remembered that this was the time of the left wing Republican Congress formed by such strong Marxists as Nora and Roddy Connolly (daughter and son of James) and George Gilmore to name but a few. The new version, which by and large is the one which is used by various organisations today, consists of seven stars positioned in the formation of the constellation on a blue background. The new flag differs from the original in more ways than the background colour. The agricultural Plough design on the flag is no longer present with only the seven stars in their original positions present forming the pattern. The new design has been attributed by some to the socialist Republican Congress though once again memories are subjective and fleeting. 'Not all the veterans of 1934 were convinced that their flag had been faithfully reproduced. One remembered that the original had shown what he described, not inaptly, as a plough ploughing up towards the stars. Others recalled a green flag with a gilt braid' (Hayes McCoy: P. 218) so again as we can see memories had reached a stage of unreliability. However the net outcome was that the new flag, despite differing ideas, should be blue and that its only representation should be the constellation. The symbolism may have been erased but at least the stars have not been forgotten.

So now we have the Starry Plough of modern times. A flag flown by numerous organisations all of whom claim some historical or ideological right of inheritance to the flag of the Irish Citizen Army, and all with certain justification. The Irish Labour Party claim a historical legacy to the starry plough and given that James Connolly was one of their founder members is perhaps their **only** claim. The modern Irish Labour Party bears no resemblance apart from the name to the party formed in 1912. It does not reflect the revolutionary socialist ideas of Connolly and is a supporter of modern capitalism despite the pretensions voiced by some of its members. One could imagine if Connolly was around today he would disown the Irish Labour Party, as he would Fianna Fail and Fine Gael. It is perhaps time the Irish Labour Party left their fantasy world claiming to be the inheritors of Connolly and state what they really are a centrist pro capitalist party. The Services, Industrial, Proffesional and Technical Union (S.I.P.T.U.) also lay a historical claim to the flag with some justification. Given the fact that when SIPTU was formed, by amalgamating a number of unions into one, its largest singular component part was the ITGWU, womb of the Citizen Army, thus giving the union a historical claim to the Starry Plough. The Irish Republican Socialist Movement lay an ideological claim to the Starry Plough which is, incidentally, the name given to the organisations newspaper. The Provisional Republican Movement also lay a similar claim as do Republican Sinn Fein for more on this see epilogue.

As memories fade and, more to the point, those who were around even at a very young age at the time the flag first appeared become themselves memories (the last surviving IRA volunteer, Dan Keating, from the war of independence died in early October 2007) it would be fair to say we may never get a definitive answer as to the authentic origins of the colours of the Irish Citizen Army.

3

REORGANISATION

As 1913 led to 1914 and the year drew on and with it the misery of the locked-out workers continued the numbers of the Citizen Army was on the decrease its membership reduced by hunger and victimization. Many who had attached themselves to the Citizen Army joined the Irish Volunteers obviously preferring, as Sean O'Casey put it, "Caitlin Ni Houlihan in respectable dress than a Caitlin in the garb of a working woman". These shifts over to the volunteers was in spite of the fact that 'the most prominent members of the executive of the volunteers were those who had done all they could to snatch from the workers the right to join the trade union of their choice; in spite of the fact that many of those who controlled or occupied positions on the local executive had locked out their employees because they had ventured to assert the first principles of Trades Unionism' (*The Story of The Irish Citizen Army* P.O' Cathasaigh P.10). Put simply they were voting to fight under the command of their oppressors, indeed Murphy himself was a nationalist MP. It would be true to say that life in the Volunteer movement was more glamorous, money for equipment was readily available because these were the volunteers of the bourgeoisie equally, certainly in the long term, as much an enemy of the working class as were the forces of occupation, in fact more so because these were Irishmen and women whom better would be expected. The Volunteers had virtually full control of all the available halls in Dublin, with the exception of the Fianna Hall in Camden street which was placed at the disposal of the Citizen Army by Constance Markievicz. All attempts by the Citizen Army to procure a hall from the Volunteers were met with a polite but firm no. In other words the more affluent Volunteers were determined to maintain their monopoly on these facilities. By March 1914 it, The Citizen Army, had been reduced to little, if any, more than a single company. Just as Captain Jack White was giving up hope Sean O'Casey suggested to him 'that definite steps should be taken to form the Citizen Army into a symbolic unit of labour, that a constitution should be drafted and submitted to a general meeting of workers; that the army should be reorganised, and a council elected' (ibid). The council would be responsible, among other matters, for the revival of systematic drills, to open a fund in order to procure equipment, to arrange for public meetings, to form companies of the army wherever labour was at its strongest and 'to generally take steps to improve and strengthen the condition and, widen the scope of the Irish Citizen Army' (O'Cathasaigh: P. 12). At a preliminary meeting attended by James Connolly, Constance Markievicz, William Partridge and P.T. Daly presided over by Captain White with Sean O'Casey as secretary arrangements were made for a public meeting to be held at Liberty Hall on March 22nd. At the meeting, this time presided over by Jim Larkin, who announced that the army would have a standard uniform and a constitution (the Army's first) which was drafted by Sean O'Casey and adopted. It declared that 'the first and last principle of the Irish Citizen Army is the avowal that the ownership of Ireland, moral and material, is vested of right in the people of Ireland, that the army stood for the absolute unity of Irish nationhood and supported the rights and liberties of the democracies of all nations' (Nevin ed. P. 259).

The first four principles of the Irish Citizen Army were, 1) 'That the first and last principal of the Irish Citizen Army is the avowal that the ownership of Ireland, moral and material, is vested of right in the people of Ireland. 2) That the Irish Citizen Army shall stand for the absolute unity of Irish nationhood and shall support the rights and liberties of the democracies of all nations. 3) That one of its objects shall be to sink all differences of birth, property and creed under the common name of Irish people. 4) That the Citizen Army shall be given to all who accept the principle of equal rights and opportunities for the Irish people' (O'Cathasaigh P.14). I find a certain contradiction in article two of the constitution because "absolute unity of Irish nationhood" must surely include the Irish exploiting class! Larkin, quite rightly, suggested that every applicant, if applicable, must be a member of their trade union. An Army Council was elected with the following as officers: Chairman Captain White, Vice-Chairmen, Jim Larkin, P.T. Daly, W. Partridge, Thomas Foran, Francis Sheehy-Skeffington, Honorary Secretary, Sean O'Casey and Honorary Treasurers, Richard Brannigan and Countess Markievicz. Surprisingly James Connolly was not a member of the first Army Council. Shortly after this meeting dark green uniforms were acquired, from the store *Arnotts,* along with broad slouched hats of the same colour and were paid for by weekly instalments by the men themselves. In April of the same year the Starry Plough flag, reputedly designed by the aforementioned man called Megahy, was adopted and carried by the Irish Citizen Army for the first time at the head of a demonstration and in the same month the Dublin Trades Council officially approved of the Army. In May 1914 Captain Jack White resigned as chairman of the Army Council and Jim Larkin was elected in his place.

The Irish Citizen Army was now reorganised and, although slightly smaller in number was more efficient and certainly looked the part. With uniforms and banners plus weaponry slowly coming in they were beginning to look like a band worthy of the name Irish Citizen ARMY . As has been mentioned at around the same time as the formation of the Irish Citizen Army was the introduction onto the political scene of the Irish Volunteers. Like the Citizen Army this much larger organisation took a leaf out of Carson's book in their formation. The what is good for the goose is good for the gander philosophy was adopted by both military organisations in nationalist Ireland, meaning that if Carson can organise the Ulster Volunteers in the North against any form of Irish independence we can organise in favour of such independence. However there was much animosity between the two organisations at first particularly over political ideology with the Citizen Army emphasising the importance of the victory over capital by labour and the Volunteers placing greater importance on the national question alone, ridiculing the Irish Citizen Army by such claims as there is no room for local trades disputes in the national question, echoed by modern politicians when cutting workers living standards "in the national interest". This negative assessment may be explained by the cross class make up of the Volunteers compared with the working class constituency of the Citizen Army, with the exception of Captain White, an Ulster Protestant, and Constance Markievicz herself born a Protestant of the landed Anglo Irish caste. Both activists came from more affluent backgrounds which is no crime in itself. Most of the Volunteer officers were from the petit bourgeois and even big bourgeois strata's of society which differed sharply from the make up of the Irish Citizen Army including its officers. However there were radicals within the Volunteer movement and one such militant was, among others, Padraig Pearse who wrote in the *Irish Freedom* in 1913 "I would like to put some of our well fed citizens in the shoes of our hungry citizens just for an experiment... I would like to ask those who know that a man can live and thrive, can house, feed and educate a large family on a pound a week, to try the experiment for themselves... I am certain they will enjoy their poverty and their hunger... they will write books on how to be happy though hungry, when their children cry out for more food they will smile, when the landlord calls for the rent they will embrace him, when their house falls upon them they will thank God, when the policemen smash in their skulls they will kiss the chastising baton". Padraig Pearse was one of the seven signatories, along with James Connolly of the proclamation in 1916 and with others like Sean MacDermott and Thomas Clarke represented the revolutionary section within the Volunteer movement, increasingly becoming known as the Irish Volunteers as opposed to the National Volunteers who were equally supporting the Irish parliamentary party. They, Pearse etal, were also members of the Irish Republican Brotherhood. However the Citizen Army personnel were still generally suspicious of the Volunteers politics as a whole even if they were evolving into two camps.

At one of the opening meetings of the Volunteers in the Rotunda some Citizen Army men turned up to hear what this new crowd had to say and when, at the end of the meeting, a rendition of the anthem *God Save Ireland* (a commemorative song about the Manchester martyrs, William Philip Allen, Michael Larkin and Michael O'Brien executed in 1867) was sang with the Irish Citizen Army men intervening and singing *"God save Larkin"*. However as time passed this animosity cooled somewhat and an occasion came to pass when the Citizen Army and the Volunteers would march together (there would always be an underlying mistrust of the Volunteers by the Citizen Army and when the war of independence kicked off in 1919 under the vanguard umbrella of the re-vamped Irish Republican Army, which consisted of former Volunteers and Citizen Army men and women, who maintained their autonomous identity as Citizen Army members, these divisions were still apparent. Anybody who has seen the film *The Wind That Shakes The Barley* the scene in the republican court sums these cleavages up). The occasion for this unity was the pilgrimage to Wolfe Tone's grave at Bodenstown, Co. Kildare, on June 26th 1914 when two companies of the Irish Citizen Army, led by Jim Larkin, were warmly welcomed by Tom Clarke, the chairman of the Wolfe Tone Memorial Committee and a progressive radical thinker sympathetic to the desires and needs of the working class. Shortly after the Wolfe Tone commemoration Jim Larkin, commandant of the Irish Citizen Army and founder of the Irish Transport and General Workers Union announced his intention to leave Ireland for the United States of America. This, he said, was "to spread the aims of Irish Labour and the Citizen Army across the USA". James Connolly assumed command of the army and leadership of the union.

The Citizen Army despite its appearance and smart uniforms were still short of weaponry despite the trickle which had found its way in their direction. The outbreak of World War One was to transform this situation. On the eve of the war Jim Larkin in the *Irish Worker* was calling 'on every man who believed in Ireland a nation to act now. England's need our opportunity. The men are ready. The guns must be got, and at once' (Nevin ed. P.260). The same point was made in the notes of the Citizen Army who, while recognising the possibilities of the Volunteers saw themselves as the only credible armed force in Ireland standing for the rights of the worker and the complete independence of the country. Get arms now anyhow or anywhere but get them.

4

WOMEN AND THE IRISH CITIZEN ARMY

The participation of women in the Irish Citizen Army is an essential contribution to any *"Descriptive History"* of the organisation. In common with socialist principles and ideology the Irish Citizen Army , in line with its parent the Irish Transport and General Workers Union, practiced a policy of gender equality. This was, of course, in common with James Connolly's own political outlook and as Commandant he was in prime position to ensure that women's equality with men was observed by all. From its inception there was no differentials made between men and women. This same equality rule also applied during the Easter Rising with Constance Markievicz, perhaps the most well documented of the women involved, holding the rank of Lieutenant. It would be perhaps more authentic to view the role of women in the Irish Citizen Army through the words of a female volunteer. Below are extracts from a statement made by Rose Hacket a volunteer of the time.

"It was a result of the big strike in 1913 that I first became attached to Liberty Hall. A workroom was opened to assist girls who had lost their employment as a result of the strike. Miss Delia larkin had charge of the girls working there".

"When Miss Larkin left Liberty Hall, Miss Helena Molony came to take charge, and that is when the work of the women's section of the Irish Citizen Army began in earnest. As well as the workroom, which was very small, we had a shop at Liberty hall. In the workroom we made most of the articles that were for sale in the shop Jinny Shanahan, who is dead, (sic) was there then. We carried on between the workshop and shop, making whatever stuff was given to us. Miss Molony was in charge of the workroom and shop. As a matter of fact, to keep us going - I don't know whether Mr Connolly or Miss Molony was responsible we made those grey-backed shirts and a lot of them went to the post office garrison. Coming near that time we held them back in case they would be required".

"I was alone in the shop the day it was raided. I had heard that from very early that morning, raids were being carried out on printing places and that they were being continued in shops. Premises in Caple Street where the *Gaelic Press* was printed had been raided. In the shop we served *The spark, Nation* (authors italics) and all those advanced papers that other shops would not sell. That morning, I had sold a copy of one of these papers to a man, who told me that shops were being raided. I said they wont get anything here. He was only gone when the police came".

"When the police entered the shop, they asked for the papers. I said wait till I get the head. I told the men in the printing office that the police were in the shop on a raid, and that Connolly was to be got. Connolly was in, and they had him down in a jiffy. The policeman was behind the counter. Connolly rushed down as quickly as he could, he just saw them with the papers and said: Drop them or I will drop you, Helena must have come in, as she was standing at the fireplace with her weapon ready, in case Connolly was attacked. She always had a gun and was always prepared. When Connolly said: Drop them or I will drop you, he had them covered from that on. The police went off and came back later with a warrant. They searched around, but they found nothing. I had hidden the stuff".

"As a result of the raid, there was a general mobilization of the Citizen Army. It was believed that there would be an attack on the place, on account of Connolly being armed during the raid. As there was a lot of ammunition and stuff being made at Liberty Hall, it would have been serious, at that stage, if it were to be seized. For the rest of that evening I could see Citizen

Army men, in their working clothes, coming from all directions of the city to the Hall. From that date until the Rising, there was a continuous guard kept on the premises. I would calculate that the raid took place about three weeks before the Rising". The role which was played by women in both the Dublin Lockout and the Easter Rising has been, to a great extent negated. With the exception of Constance Markievicz, see below, and perhaps Maude Gonne, who was no socialist, very little appears in publication about the role played by women in the Irish struggle.

"The girls took part in night route marches with the men of the Citizen Army. We would mobilize at midnight. I took part in the one to Dublin Castle. I think I only missed one route march, which went to the North side". Rose Hacket took part in the Easter Rising and was stationed at St. Stephens Green under the command of Michael Mallin and Constance Markievicz. With the evacuation of the Green she was in the College of Surgeons for the duration. This is where she was stationed when the surrender was accepted by Michael Mallin. Rose Hacket finishes off her statement with a very important, and again neglected point. "Historically, Liberty hall is the most important building that we have in the city. Yet it is not thought of at all by most people. More things happened there, in connection with the Rising, than any other place. It really started from there" (Extracts from statement by Miss Rose Hacket member of womens section Irish Citizen Army: W/S 546 courtesy of National Archives). Rose Hacket, as far as my research can reveal, would have been representative of many working class women involved in both the Dublin Lockout and Easter Rising. Unlike Constance Markievicz she came from a working class background and had nothing to lose but her chains. However this observation is not intended to take anything away from either because class background can not be helped. It is commitment which is the defining factor and both had plenty of this.

The medical department was organised and coordinated by a member of the female gender, Dr Kathleen Lynn. Dr Lynn often held lectures on first aid and field dressing which during the course of future events would prove to be of utmost value to the Citizen Army. These lectures and demonstrations on elementary first-aid were given to both men and women members of the Citizen Army in an environment of unison and were psychologically uplifting in so far as they bound together the men and women volunteers irrespective of gender. When Captain Sean Connolly was shot during an engagement with the enemy around the City Hall it was Dr Lynn, who was part of his command, who tended his wounds. Unfortunately due to the severity of his injuries there was little she could do and he unfortunately succumbed to his injuries and died. The women's section as a whole was under the control of Dr Lynn, Helena Molony, who was to replace Delia Larkin managing the workshop, Constance Markievicz, and Miss Ffrench-Mullen. The lectures conducted by Dr Lynn and Miss Ffrench-Mullen were very much responsible for adapting the women members for their future roles and tasks in the Citizen Army.

During the Easter Rising women members of the Irish Citizen Army suffered in ways which perhaps only women can often never receiving the recognition they deserved, despite the equality policy. One incident, no doubt among many, involving Miss Chris Caffrey, a young member of the womens section, who had been sent by Commandant Mallin with a dispatch to the GPO but failed to get through. Frank Robbins gives an account of what she told him of the incident in his book *Under The Starry Plough*. 'She had been carrying dispatches from Mallin to the GPO and Jacobs Factory since Easter Monday. Her dress suggested a young war widow and she added to that impression by wearing a red, white and blue badge. She set off as usual with her dispatch that Thursday morning and some of the unfriendly people in the area noticed her leaving the College of Surgeons. They tailed her through various side streets into Dame Street and when they saw some British soldiers they denounced her as a spy. She was accosted by two officers and questioned. Her replies did not satisfy them and she was asked to accompany them into Trinity College for further interrogation. She made no demur and knowing the tight spot she was in decided to try and bluff her way out of her predicament. On the way through the gates of Trinity she put the dispatch in her mouth and began chewing it. One of the officers saw gesture and immediately asked her what she had put in her mouth. Without a moments hesitation she replied "a sweet", and taking a paper bag of sweets from her pocket asked him if he would like one. The officer refused abruptly.

The officers then took her into a room and informed her they proposed to search her. She protested tearfully expostulating that it was a poor tribute to the memory of her late husband who had "given his life for the empire". They were not convinced and seeing this she demanded to be searched by one of her own sex. They were sorry, they retorted, to be unable to accommodate her with a woman searcher and proposed to do the job themselves. Without going into details Chris assured me that they did a thorough job of work' (Robbins:P118).

Obviously the British impression of being chivalrous as suggested in the case of sparing the life of Constance Markievicz after the Easter Rising did not apply in this and countless other instances. It is a harrowing experience for any person to be strip searched but what of course made the case of Chris Caffrey more horrific and degrading was the fact that she was a woman searched by men. Chris Caffrey's case was probably one of many incidents of abuse suffered by the female population of Dublin during the rebellion, both combatants and non combatants alike. In such circumstances it is not unusual, though no less wrong, for personnel from the stronger military power to take advantage of the situation in attempts at degradation which is in turn aimed at sapping moral.

5

THE OUTBREAK OF WAR

The first world war, 1914-1918, was a war between two imperialist gangs of thieves. Unlike the latter variant of World War Two it could in no way be described a war of ideologies which the events of 1939-1945 could arguably have been. In this respect during the years spanning 1914-1918 no working class person irrespective of nationality should have gone out to slaughter their class brethren. This was an issue which was to split the second international with many socialists, despite once arguing to the contrary, queuing up to support their indigenous bourgeoisie and monarchies. This act of class betrayal disgusted revolutionary socialists like James Connolly and VI Lenin, even though they never met, with the latter proclaiming "down with the Second International" forward towards the Third International. Unlike the Second World War which was arguably for many a war against Fascism world war one could in no way be categorized in this description as it was a conflict between, initially, two healthy capitalist monarchies and their allies. The execution of the Austrian Arch Duke Franz Ferdinand by Serbian nationalists was a convenient excuse for the major powers to go to war with each other. Initially Austria declared war on Serbia with Russia, traditional defenders of the Slavs, coming in on the side of the Serbs. Germany entered alongside Austria and France with Russia. Britain was initially not involved but needed an excuse to become so. They were concerned about their trade routes to the empire so when Germany invaded Belgium they invoked some obscure treaty in defence of the small country, the "right of small nations to self determination" (which apparently did not include Ireland's right to the same) . The invasion of Belgium by Germany was a convenient excuse to become involved by Britain to check the rise in German naval power and capitalist expansion and utilize her empire troops. On the side of imperial Germany were the Austro/Hungarian Empire, the Ottoman Empire along with other less grandeur sounding countries hoping in the event of victory to claim a few spoils. Lined up beside the British Empire were France, the Russian Empire, Italy, Belgium, Japan and later on the United States of America. The causes of the first world war, despite what historians would have us believe had, as we have mentioned, very little to do with the Austrian Arch Duke Franz Ferdinand being assassinated in Sarajevo by Serbian nationalists or the right of "small nations" following Germany's invasion of Belgium. One of the main causes behind the outbreak of the first world war was and the mass slaughter of working class people which took place was one capitalist and rapidly industrialising country, Germany, gaining ground both economically and militarily on the established industrial and military power Britain. Germany was also catching up in the race for superiority on the high seas something which for centuries had been a British preserve. The working class combatants of both competing armies stood to gain absolutely nothing and had everything to lose, their lives. It is worthy of note that the monarchies involved were all related. For example the British King and German Kaiser were cousins as was the Russian Tsar.

Even though conscription was not applicable in Ireland at the offset of the war, and ultimately never was despite many threats to the contrary, Connolly among others was ever mindful of the possibility. He also saw an opportunity at some point for Ireland and the Citizen Army to exploit England's difficulty in pursuit of her own self determination and the right of this "small nation". It was unlikely that Ireland would ever be offered another open opportunity to exploit as this.

At the outbreak of the war James Connolly was in Belfast pondering the implications of the conflict, he was determined that the opportunity should not pass without a blow being struck for Irish freedom. The outbreak of hostilities cannot have surprised Connolly, he never took his finger off the political pulse, but the attitude to the war of his socialist colleagues from the second international in the belligerent countries did. Their failure to oppose the war appalled him as one by one these former comrades, the Russian delegation exempted and even this was split on factional lines , fell over each other in the stampede to support their native bourgeoisie and monarchies. He wrote in the *Irish Worker* of 8th August 'should the working class of Europe, rather than slaughter each other for the benefit of kings and financiers, proceed tomorrow to erect barricades all over Europe …that war might be abolished, we should be perfectly justified in following such a glorious example and contributing our aid to the final dethronement of the vulture classes that rule and rob the world' (Nevin ed. P.261). The First World War also split the Volunteer movement into two factions. One faction, by far the larger of the two was to follow John Redmond, Nationalist MP and leader of the Home Rule Movement, who urged the Volunteers to join in the war and fight for the British empire. This was under the thinly veiled promise from the British government that a limited form of Home Rule would be granted after hostilities with Germany had ceased. However Redmond was warned by that same government that although a form of Home Rule would almost certainly be forthcoming he, Redmond, must remember what they, the government, had promised Carson in the North. The body of Volunteers who went off to the slaughter became known as the National Volunteers while those who stayed behind in Ireland, as conscription had not been introduced, retained the name Irish Volunteers. Connolly taunted Redmond with the following teaser " *Full steam ahead, John Redmond said that all is well chum, Home Rule will come when we are dead and buried out in Belgium*". It is clear that Connolly saw the war as an opportunity for Ireland to strike a blow for freedom and he had a large banner draped across Liberty Hall declaring 'WE SERVE NEITHER KING NOR KAISER BUT IRELAND'. The Irish Citizen Army were servants to neither the British or German empires.

With Redmond leading the national Volunteers off to the slaughter as second class soldiers in the British army, second class, because unlike their Ulster counterparts who were formed into the 36th Ulster Division and flew their own colours and had their own officers with Catholics strictly forbidden, the National Volunteers were forced to march under the Union Jack only. The National Volunteers numbered around 180,000 men and were by far the larger section of the once united Irish Volunteers. About 18,000 of these remained at home and maintained the name Irish Volunteers under the leadership of Eoin MacNeill, who was to be greatly responsible for the defeat at Easter week in 1916. Redmond and MacNeill could be held largely responsible for the failure of the rising though MacNeill chiefly because Redmond, as the leader of the nationalist Home Rule party, was not expected to be a revolutionary whereas the aforementioned had delusions to this aim.

The Irish Citizen Army could only arm and equip around 200 personnel but had they the weaponry there is little doubt they could have armed upwards of 2,000. With the outbreak of war in August 1914 military and police repression increased. On December 4th 1914 a force of military and DMP smashed the printing press of *The Irish Worker*, the organ of the ITGWU, and thus suppressed the unions paper which also gave expression to the Irish Citizen Army. Other Irish nationalist publications were also to fall victim of these repressive measures and among those numbered were *Sinn Fein* and *Irish Freedom*. Connolly managed to get a successor to *The Irish Worker* called *The Worker* which he had printed by the Socialist Labour Press in Glasgow. This was a temporary arrangement until the printing plant was re- installed at Liberty Hall where *The Workers Republic* was founded.

One of the main reasons MacNeill held the Irish Volunteers back from Redmond's pact with genocide was to combat the threat of conscription. Rumours had been rife about conscription being introduced to Ireland for quite some time and an anti-conscription committee was formed during the Summer of 1915. To this committee Connolly commented: 'We will not be asked to accept conscription by the British Government unless the British ruling class has made up its mind that only conscription can save the Empire. If it does make up its mind to that measure it will enforce conscription though every river in Ireland runs red with blood' (Berresford Ellis: P. 217). The Dublin Trades Council also passed a resolution proposed by a member of the Irish Volunteers, Peadar Macken, opposing conscription and urging workers to join either the Citizen Army or the Irish Volunteers.

The leadership of the Volunteers sought some form of co-operation with the Dublin Trades Council, though why only Dublin is unclear perhaps because it was the largest centre of industry, to resist the actions of the employers trying to force their workers into the army. This co-operation should have been sought through the Irish Trades Union Congress (ITUC) which covered the whole country and not just Dublin. Meetings took place between the Irish Volunteers and the Dublin Trades Council and among those representing the Volunteers were Eoin MacNeill, Padraic Pearse and Sean MacDiarmada while James Connolly, Thomas Foran and William O'Brien represented the Trades Council. Connolly wanted the Volunteers to support, militarily, any action which the workers may take against the employers regarding their tactics of coercing workers into joining the British army. This was rejected, particularly by MacNeill, who even at this early stage was showing signs of his political shallowness and class loyalty to the employers. If he could not endorse this simple request he could hardly be expected to support the notion of a rebellion at a later stage.

In 1915 the British Government introduced the "Defence Of the Realm Act", DORA. This act provided for the commandeering of any factory or workers which it deemed necessary for war work. The regulations of DORA were also very far reaching and included, among other points, the power to try by courts-martial those not subject to military law and was used against civilians in Egypt as well as Ireland. It was these regulations which were used to court-martial and execute the sixteen men after the Easter Rising. DORA was sometimes used for the slightest infringement or suspicion of such on person or persons thought by the authorities to be a threat to the Empire. The act was used to obtain a search warrant for Liberty Hall and other premises suspected of printing and/or retailing subversive literature. Under war time conditions the definition of the word subversive took on a whole new meaning, especially in Ireland. The act was applicable in Britain as well as Ireland and throughout the Empire. It was used to outlaw strikes in Britain though this had the opposite effect because it gave rise to a more militant shop stewards movement which defied the class collaborationist union leadership in calling unofficial strike action to further the interests of the working class. These conditions also gave rise to other rank and file initiatives such as "The National Minorities Movement" which, like the shop stewards committees operated without the sanctioning of the trade union leadership. It proved more trouble than it was worth to use DORA against these movements as production would have ground to a halt. However in Ireland the British Government did not have the same reservations about applying the regulations available under the act, perhaps because they always felt there was a revolutionary tendency waiting for the opportune moment.

In January 1916 conscription was introduced in England, Scotland Wales and Cornwall (the old Cornish Parliament, the Stannary was never and has never been legally dissolved) but not in Ireland. An attempt to introduce conscription into Ireland would not be made until 1918 when the war was nearly at an end. This attempt by Lord French was resisted and repelled. However it could be reasonably argued that this effort by French was the main reason for the electoral success of Sinn Fein in the General election in December of that year and perhaps not, as is wildly promoted, out of sympathy for the executed men of 1916, though this was a contributing factor.

Connolly could see the opportunities which arose out of England's difficulties for Ireland. However he was not the only person, or persons, who saw the outbreak of war as an opportunity, but for totally unparalleled reasons. Many of the men who, all be it foolishly, went off to fight for the empire, the same empire which had subjugated them for centuries, left behind wives and families. The war was to destroy many of these families in more ways than one. Firstly, and obviously, if the man of the family was killed it deprived the wife of a husband and the children a father. Secondly the wives who were left behind by their soldier husbands received an allowance from the government for loss of income, or potential income. This allowance was known as "separation" money and the women were called "separation women" or, sometimes "separation widows" which, the reader should not misunderstand that the latter term reflected the fact that the husband had been killed in action as to this it, as a generic term, bore no relevance. Separation money was received whether the husband had been killed in action or was alive and fighting in the trenches. Some of these women wished the war would continue for ever as they were financially better off under these conditions as they got money which they would not receive if their husband was at home and unemployed which would have been the case in the majority of instances. To add insult to injury some of these women, and this also happened in Britain, struck up sexual relationships with other men at home while their husbands were away. Some of these men were the sweaters and grinders, employers, of those men who happened to be in work when war broke out had promised the man a place in their employment on his return from the front. Not all the women were sleeping with their husbands former or potential employers, in fact it would be fair to say not even a significant minority, but never the less it happened and this happened in all the belligerent countries. The women who did not practice this unfaithful act regarded those who did, or were known to, with utter contempt.

With the outbreak of the Easter Rising it was the "separation women" who were to the fore in opposition to the event. They were fiercely against the insurrection on two fronts. First, and in most cases the more relevant, was the fact that because of the occupation of the General Post Office by the rebel forces they could not get their "separation" money. At this they were most put out and hurled verbal insults at the insurgents and could not wait till the soldiers came and arrested them all. The second reason, and by far the least important in most cases, was that this bunch, the rebels, were causing trouble at home while their men were out in Flanders fighting and in many cases getting slaughtered at the front. If these would be soldiers wanted to fight nobody was preventing them, in fact their wives would probably appreciate the "separation" money, so why did they not do the "honourable" thing and go to the front? This assumption that "their wives would appreciate" the "separation" money was, of course pure fallacy. The wives of the insurgents, if not in favour of their husbands fighting in the rebellion were even more opposed to their men going off to fight Britain's war at the front, however this reality did not deter the "separation women" from making such things up.

Connolly despaired at the pathetic sight of these women screaming outside the GPO for their money and an attempt was made to distribute the said mode of exchange before hostilities with the crown began. Why could these poor creatures not see that their men should at least not be at the front fighting not only another countries war, but also a war which would only benefit one class of person irrespective of the outcome on the battlefield, and if at home these same men should be fighting for their own class, the working class and thus their country. However such sensible arguments as those which Connolly was passing through his mind would have been wasted on these screaming women who, given the chance, perhaps would have preferred to tear the insurgents limb from limb. The events just described were comparatively mild compared with some of the things which occurred during Easter week. From screaming "separation women", which was one thing and almost understandable though not condonable, wide spread looting became the order of the day when any lull in the fighting between the rebels and British forces occurred. This caused the leadership, and particularly Connolly more despair as even firing volleys over the looters heads failed to make any real impact in stemming the looting. The hostility shown by the majority of the general population towards the insurgents prevailed right up to the surrender of the Republican forces after one week of heroic fighting. As they were been marched by the victors through the streets of Dublin some civilians threw such missiles as decaying fruit at them chamber pots of urine and rotten eggs, and these were the very same people the rising was supposed to liberate.

6

RECREATION

This may be an appropriate opportunity to familiarise the reader with the social side of Citizen Army membership. It was not solely about drilling, parading, weaponry training etc., this routine was sometimes broken on a Sunday for recreation. Most Sunday evenings popular concerts were held at Croydon Park, Fairview in North Dublin during the Summer months. These concerts were very popular with members of the Citizen Army, their wives, girlfriends, friends and relatives. 'Dancing, singing and piping kept the night perpetually young, and, after a hard weeks work of drilling, parading and routine duties, these gatherings were a welcome change, when discipline was relaxed, and the officers remembered they were human and joined hilariously in the fun and frolic of the moment' (*Story Of The Irish Citizen Army* P.36). These recreational evenings were essential for the maintenance of moral in the ranks of the Irish Citizen Army. Jim Larkin, shy as he sometimes was in such circumstances, would after some coaxing entertain his audience with a rendition of The Red Flag and the Rising Of The Moon amongst many other popular revolutionary verse. During the same period James Connolly would have been busy writing labour songs, many of which are collated in The *James Connolly Song Book* still available today.

Many other features were introduced to these Sunday evenings of merriment, for example the five mile marathon which proved to be embarrassingly successful. Another event which was very popular was the Citizen Army assault on a cowboy stockade, with the advancing army taking cover and firing as they advanced. The event consisted of a mock attack on a lonely outpost of cowboys by red Indians. The result was that the Indians always won by wiping out the stockade with fire. While the Indians were celebrating their victory the Citizen Army representing the US Cavalry in turn took them by surprise, revenged the men who had been killed by the Indians and wiped them out (perhaps the Citizen Army should have represented the Indians wiping out the colonial occupiers). The men posing as Indians were members of the National Guard which was a breakaway group from the Fianna, the junior section of the Volunteers. This event obviously had connotations for the same army back in what we call for some strange reason the real world. Everybody looked forward to these Sunday evenings when bands played, artistes sang and children danced. When the weather was bad concerts were held in Liberty Hall. So life in the Irish Citizen Army was not solely about monotony and preparing for the victory of labour over capital, though this theme was never far from the pivotal topic of the entertainment. The moral here is that all work and no play makes for a pretty boring existence which the Citizen Army leadership were well aware. Therefore the Sunday evenings of merriment were strongly encouraged. The Irish Citizen Army also took part in drilling competitions as part of their recreational activities, activities which were very useful for boosting moral. Their turn out was generally regarded as second to none as time after time they won first prize awards for their dress and drilling. It was almost expected in these competitions that if the Citizen Army, the army of the proletariat, were taking part they would invariably take first prize, over the more middle class Volunteers.

7

Plans For A United Front

Any country which had been subjugated for the length of time Ireland had would feel inclined to take advantage of the oppressors predicament such as that now faced by Britain with their involvement in the first world war. Unfortunately many of these countries although feeling inclined to rebel against the rule of the crown failed to seize the initiative due to the fact that they lacked the personnel capable of giving the correct leadership. This applied to those countries under the yolk of Britannia and others which were suffering under the rule of other imperialist countries such as the heel of the Austro/Hungarian Empire, the German Empire and others. Many of these countries had a strong revolutionary current running through the population but no leadership worthy of thought. In Ireland, however, there were currents capable of giving a lead and James Connolly was one of them. He was not alone as events were to reveal but equally as the same events were also to make apparent support among the populace for a rebellion against British rule was tepid to say the least. Evidence of this level of support would become apparent when the insurgents were finally defeated and marched through the streets of Dublin. The reception they received was not one, certainly initially, of applause and cheers as would have been expected. Boos and insults were among the milder expressions of disapproval the baying mobs felt fit to voice. Only when the executions of the leaders began did the mood of the population begin to swing in the direction of support for the rebellion which had taken place.

Connolly had been toying with the idea of a united front comprising of the Irish Citizen Army and Irish Volunteers (the latter had split into two factions over whether to support Britain's war effort or not. One faction, the largest, had supported the

Irish party MP and leader John Redmond and gone to sacrifice themselves for the crown under some vague promise that Home Rule would be considered on their return. The other faction who retained the name Irish Volunteers had stayed at home under the leadership of Eoin MacNeill). An opportunity for such joint action was soon to present itself when plans were made for eighty Volunteers and forty Citizen Army men to seize the Mansion House in a bid to prevent British Prime Minister Herbert Asquith addressing a recruiting meeting there. Unfortunately the event had to be abandoned but on the same night one hundred Citizen Army men with rifles marched from Liberty Hall to Stephens Green where a vast opposition meeting was being addressed by Constance Markievicz. Co-operation between the two organisations was gelling. After Larkin's departure for the USA in October 1914 James Connolly took charge as Commandant with Michael Mallin as Chief of Staff. Connolly maintained links with militants in the Volunteers like Pearse but he was determined to ensure the Citizen Army remained an independent force. Part of the plan of Connolly's to maintain these links was joint group and individual action against the Crown. One early example of possible joint group action is briefly mentioned above but there was also individual joint action, particularly in the field of sabotage.

Martin King was a member of the Irish Citizen Army 1915-1916 and below is a brief statement of such individual joint action with the Volunteers he was involved in: "I was employed as a cable joiner in the Post Office Service and, on that account, was familiar with the layout of all telephone and telegraph cables.

In the latter part of 1915, James Connolly asked me, if he wanted to cut communications with England, how would he set about it?. I told him he could cut them at Talbot Street or Lombard Street. He asked me if I knew these places and, if I could do the job. I told him that, if there was anything I didn't know, my foreman, Andy Fitzpatrick, who was a Volunteer would be able to tell me. He told me to pick up all the information I could on this matter. About this time I gave my official pass card to James Connolly. With this card admission could be gained to all government offices and buildings. I believe it was afterwards used for this purpose. I had considerable difficulty in obtaining a replacement card.

On Good Friday morning, 1916, Andy Fitzpatrick brought me on a tour of the principal trunk line centres with a view to the disruption of communications on Easter Sunday. The places visited were Kevin Street, which carried the Wexford and Waterford trunk line, the canal bank near Potobello Bridge, where a pole carried the same trunk lines, a pole near Bolands Mills on Grand Canal which carried Wexford and Newcastle lines. The cross channel telegraph cables came in at Newcastle. We came in at Brunswick Street and examined the cables at the corner of Lombard Street. The cables there connected to underground wires from Newcastle to Westland Row. There was, in this cable, a special wire between Dublin Castle and London. We decided that the cables should be cut at this point. We came from Lombard Street to Palace Street and inspected the box there. These were mostly police wires to all the city stations. In the afternoon we visited Talbot Street, where the cross channel telephone cables pass under-ground. We decided that the Northern lines could be disrupted at Howth Junction. The underground cables in the box of Church Street Bridge, which took in the Viceregal Lodge was to be cut.

A meeting of volunteers, at which a volunteer officer presided, was held at Frederick Street and was attended by my brothers, George, Sam, Arthur and myself, of the Citizen Army". (statement by Martin King, member of the Irish Citizen Army 1915-1916. Subject: Plans for disruption of communications, Easter 1916. W/S 543, courtesy National Archives). This is one example of joint individual action on sabotage which took place by members of the Citizen Army and the Irish Volunteers, who co-ordinated perfectly for the task. The ultimate joint group action by the two organisations is outlined below.

The Citizen Army under Connolly's stewardship stood for revolution, preferably though not exclusively socialist revolution, which was always Connolly's first preference and ultimate goal. However revolutionary situations are not always ala carte. In the last issue of the *Irish Worker* before its suppression in December 1914 Connolly threw down the challenge: 'A resurrection! Aye, out of the grave of the first Irishman murdered for protesting against Irelands participation in this thrice-accursed war there will rise anew the Spirit of Irish Revolution' (Nevin ed. P.262). How to exploit Britain's problems in the European war was to be constantly at the forefront of Connolly's mind, this war surely gave Ireland an opportunity to take advantage of her centuries old tormentors conundrum. The question was which way to proceed? Connolly wrote in the *Irish Worker*, now published clandestinely, in the issue of 30th October 1915 the position of the Irish Citizen Army, 'the first publicly organised armed citizen force south of the Boyne, whose constitution pledged its members to work for an Irish Republic and for the emancipation of labour. He saw it as the army of a class whose aims went much further than the achievement of national freedom', but also the emancipation of the proletariat. For Connolly national freedom alone constituted bourgeois freedom alone offering the working class little, if anything of any consequence. The way he viewed things were that the workers of Ireland had fought as part of the armies led by their masters, and masters of other countries at that, but never as members of an army officered, trained and inspired by men of their own class and land. Now the object was, with arms in their hands, to steer their own course, to carve out their own destiny and neither Home Rule, nor lack of Home Rule would make them lay down their arms

.

8

JOINT ACTION

Connolly was now thinking of joint action on a larger scale in the field with the Volunteers to exploit Britain's present difficulties on the European front. He constantly questioned in his mind the commitment of the Volunteer movement and was soon to find positive answers to his concerns. Between January 19/22, 1916, he met with the revolutionary elements of the Volunteers, all of whom were members of the secret Irish Republican Brotherhood (IRB) and led by Padraic Pearse. The IRB organised separately and without the knowledge of the official Volunteer leadership presided over by Eoin MacNeill. The meeting Connolly had with the IRB leadership was shrouded, for obvious reasons, in secrecy and even leading members of his own union and the Citizen Army were unaware of the event. So much was the secrecy surrounding this meeting that on the surface it appeared that the IRB had kidnapped Connolly, a possible version still believed by many to this day. Frank Robbins states in his book *Under The Starry Plough*, regarding the kidnapping of Connolly story, 'the fact that he freely became a member of the Irish Republican Brotherhood from the date of the meeting is a clear indication that the story of his kidnapping was a myth' (P:73-74). Connolly was not the kind of man who would have submitted to being held against his will and the kidnapping myth remains exactly that, a myth. In his last article, What Is Our Programme, which he wrote before the meeting at which he came to an agreement with the Military Council of the IRB to set a date for a rising against the British, "the time for Irelands battle is now... it is our duty... to strengthen the hand of those of the leaders who are for action...we are neither rash nor cowardly. We know our opportunity when we see it and we know when it has gone".

As opposed to the kidnapping theory surrounding the meeting between Connolly and the IRB it is far more probable, in fact almost certain that Pearse had learned of Connolly's plans to lead out the Citizen Army unilaterally as a means of forcing the Volunteers into action. On learning of this Pearse and Sean MacDermott had approached Connolly and urged him to hold his hand in order not to ruin plans already made. From that time on James Connolly was co-opted onto the revolutionary leadership of the IRB. Connolly has been accused by some, including Sean O'Casey, of betraying the cause of labour in favour of Irish nationalism and, it is claimed, his participation in the Easter rising is further proof of this switch. This was not necessarily the case as Connolly's first preference for an insurrection was more likely to have been a rebellion led and organised by the forces of labour. However in the absence of such an event Connolly was prepared to forfeit, at least for the time being, these aspirations in return for a place on the military council of the IRB, though he still held out hopes that once the rising had began the proletariat would perceive what was happening and the hope was they would come out numerically in support of the insurgents. The national rebellion was, to Connolly, another avenue towards socialist revolution. This theory is supported by the often quoted term "The cause of labour is the cause of Ireland, The cause of Ireland is the cause of labour", the two struggles were inseparable. What use is a free Ireland if the majority of the population, the working class, are still imprisoned by the chains of capitalism?. Connolly's participation in the Easter Rising was more an attempt to raise the consciousness of labour rather than depress it. After these events the Irish Citizen Army's preparations for the "blessed day of days" were pushed forward. Route marches became more frequent. The quest for arms intensified and Liberty Hall was under armed guard day and night. At the suggestion of Councillor William Partridge, the Council of the Irish Citizen Army resolved to hoist the green flag of Ireland over Liberty Hall. Connolly wrote "where better could that flag fly than over the unconquered citadel of the Irish working class, the fortress of the militant working class of Ireland". Connolly continued 'We are out for Ireland for the Irish. But who are the Irish? Not the rack-renting, slum-owning landlords; not the sweating, profit grinding capitalists... Not these are the Irish upon the future depends. Not these, but the Irish working class, the only secure foundation upon which a free nation can be reared. The cause of labour is the cause of Ireland, the cause of Ireland is the cause of labour. They cannot be dissevered' (Nevin ed P. 264).

The following are extracts from a statement given by Mathew Connolly, brother of Captain Sean Connolly (no relation to the Commandant) Irish Citizen Army who was in command of the City Hall Garrison, where he was killed in action.

"With about three years training in the Fianna Eireann, and at the request of my father, I joined the boys section of the Irish Citizen Army at Croydon Park Fairview in the mid-summer of 1914. On my first parade, the night of my enrolment, I was promoted section leader and given a squad of eight boys to drill. In due course we were allowed to take part in general parades and route marches, attend lectures on first aid given by Dr Kathleen Lynn, on street fighting given by James Connolly, and in target practice on the miniature rifle range in Liberty Hall.

Early in the year 1916, a special mobilization order was issued, and every man on parade was interviewed privately by Commandant James Connolly. When my turn came for the interview, I stood before Connolly, who was seated at a small table, and saluted. My father and four brothers had already been before him, and now here was another of the same family, a mere lad but feeling important. Having warned me that the answer to the following question he was about to put to me could be given at my own free will, that it was not an oath, and would not be binding in any way, he said do you promise faithfully, on your word of honour, that, if the Citizen Army have to fight alone in this coming revolution you will take your place in the ranks?. I answered yes sir I do"

The last piece of this statement could be said to highlight yet again the lingering doubts Connolly held about the volunteers. Why else would the thought that the Citizen Army may have to fight alone even enter his head if the doubt did not exist? It should be remembered that this question was asked, by Connolly, of his personnel long before Eoin MacNeill, nominal chief of the Volunteers, had any notion of the rising, however it is unclear whether it was before or after his meeting with Pearse and the other leaders of the IRB.

The Irish Citizen Army was, by now, very much a self sufficient organisation and much of their weaponry was homemade from scratch or was other weaponry improvised for the use of. "The armoury room , on the first floor, was a busy place. Improvised hand grenades were being manufactured. Cartridges were being altered, to fit rifles and guns for which they were never meant. Bayonets, of an old French type, were being heated over a blow lamp and bent or reshaped, to fit an old Mauser rifle. It was a quite common thing, on entering the armoury room, to find a man sitting over the fire brewing a can of tea on one side of it, while melting a pot of lead on the other side; two or three men at a bench, making some repairs to a rifle, while at the same time two or three others were stretched out on the floor, snoring fast asleep". Mathew Connolly was assigned to the same garrison as his brother, and commanding officer, Sean at the City Hall. "The general mobilisation was called for that afternoon at three O'clock. Headed by James Connolly, Mallin and Countess Markievicz, the entire Citizen Army made a tour of the principal city streets, and returned to the Hall at about five O'clock, where we lined up, Connolly addressed us, saying that we were no longer the Citizen Army, that we had merged with the Volunteers, under the title Irish Republican Army" (Extracts from witness statement by Mathew Connolly, brother of Captain Sean Connolly, ICA, subject ICA 1914-1916; Easter week 1916. Courtesy of National Archives W/S 1,746). This, as has been mentioned, was the public position of James Connolly regarding to what amounted to a merger with the Volunteers under the name Irish Republican Army. However it flies in the face of his private address to the Citizen Army "In the event of victory hold on to your rifles, as those with whom we are fighting may stop before our goal is reached. We are out for economic as well as political liberty". This was the theory of continuous revolution put in lay mans terms. Further evidence of the Irish Citizen Army's continued autonomy would be exampled when the surrender was issued, April 30th, it was signed by Pearse as Commandant of the Volunteers but signed separately by James Connolly leader of the Citizen Army.

The rising was to go ahead on April 24th 1916, though originally scheduled for Sunday 23rd and on the evening of Palm Sunday, after the hoisting of the green flag over the citadel, Connolly addressed the Citizen Army. 'The odds are a thousand to one against us, but in the event of victory, hold on to your rifles, as those with whom we are fighting may stop before our goal is reached. We are out for economic as well as political liberty. Hold on to your rifles' Connolly repeated. He was referring to Pearse and the other members of the IRB and not MacNeill and his cohorts because by now it was obvious they were not going to be involved in the rising. They were, therefore, no longer part of the equation. This would be further evidence that although Connolly had gone into a kind of partnership with the Volunteers and the IRB leadership, as a revolutionary socialist primarily he could still not be blinded from the shallow political limitations, radical as they may have been, of the accompanying organisation. However on Easter Monday, April 24th, 1916 Padraic Pearse with the Commandant of the Irish Citizen Army, James Connolly, by his side read aloud the proclamation of the Irish Republic from the steps of the General Post Office in O'Connell Street Dublin. The union of action between the Irish Citizen Army and the Irish Volunteers was complete at least for the duration of the insurrection. However as Connolly led the Citizen Army out of Liberty Hall with his loyal secretary Winfred Carney at his side, as has been aforementioned his reservations about the long term aims of the Irish Volunteers were voiced. By the same token publicly Connolly stated again "there are no longer an Irish Citizen Army and Irish Volunteers but one Irish Republican Army". This could well have been more for public consumption than a reflection of Connolly's private political thoughts.

***

This may be a suitable point to inform the reader of the inventiveness and pragmatism of James Connolly and the Irish Citizen Army. One of the first positions of capture on Monday 24th April was the taking of the school of wireless telegraphy at the corner of O'Connell Street and Lower Abbey Street. Here was a ships transmitter which had been out of action since the beginning of the war. This transmitter was repaired by Citizen Army technicians and restored to working order. This enabled the insurgents to transmit messages to the outside world, a privilege enjoyed only by the British forces up until this restoration. The makeshift radio station was ready for transmission by Tuesday 25th April and was the first station in Ireland known to broadcast illegally. Messages reached as far as the USA and such statements as **REVOLUTION IN IRELAND** and **REVOLT IN IRELAND** were received in the United States a considerable time before the official version of events came through from London. However by Wednesday transmission became impossible and the transmitter was carried across the road in an upturned table under heavy fire from British troops to the GPO. It is thought the transmitter perished in the fire at the Post Office when the building was burnt down and the rising crushed.

***

Prior to the Rising the now famous aforementioned Proclamation of the Republic was being printed in Liberty Hall under the armed guard of the Citizen Army. The reason for the armed guard had nothing to do with the printers and compositors, Michael Molloy, Liam O'Brien and Christopher Joseph Brady, trying to escape. Brady was first introduced to James Connolly in1915 at Liberty Hall by Patrick Daly who was a compositor. Brady was the foreman in charge of two compositors, these were the aforementioned, Michael Molloy and Liam O'Brien, and these three men were to print the proclamation. They also printed the *Workers Republic* and union membership cards for the Irish Transport and General Workers Union.

The following is an extract from a statement written by Christopher Brady: " On Good Friday James Connolly told me to call to his office as he wanted to see me very privately. I went to his office and he told me that he was speaking to my colleagues, Michael Molloy and William O'Brien, and he asked me if I could be in Liberty Hall with them on Easter Sunday morning between 10 and 11am. He didn't say what he wanted us for. He met us on the steps of Liberty Hall on Easter Sunday morning, brought us upstairs to one of the rooms and introduced us to Tomas McDonagh. James Connolly said these are my workmen here. Then Tomas McDonagh said to us, well men, the time is about opportune to strike a blow for Ireland. He said, I will read to you first the manuscript which I want you to produce in print. When he had read it over to us he handed it over to us he handed me the manuscript (sic) first to read and when I had read it he asked me to pass it on to my two colleagues. When he had finished reading he asked for a decision. I said, as a humble workman I consider it a great honour to be entrusted to do such a heroic job. The others answered in a similar manner. When I read the document I fully understood that it was a document proclaiming an Irish Republic and that it meant war, but my colleagues and myself were unanimous in our decision. Tomas McDonagh said, if we can hold out in this fight in order that Irelands voice can be heard at the peace conference and you boys will not be forgotten. McDonagh then said to Connolly, James will you have those men sworn in. Connolly replied, no, I will vouch for those men's secrecy". This could or, perhaps was, to maintain the men's civilian status and to give the impression that, if the hall was raided by the authorities they were working under duress. Also in the unfortunate event of a raid and, which was extremely unlikely, the men broke under interrogation they were under no added pressure of breaking an oath.

Brady continues, "The machine was ready for first printing at about 8.30 on Easter Sunday night and the job was finished between 12 and 1 on Easter Monday morning. We had run off 2,500 copies. I gave the first proof to James Connolly at 9pm and he checked it with the manuscript and I never saw the manuscript after that. During the printing progress the Citizen Army were as usual guarding the machine room. Lieutenant William Partridge was in charge" (Extracts from statement Christopher J. Brady 3rd July 1952 Courtesy National Archives). Even though the Citizen Army normally guarded the machine room, should Liberty Hall be paid a visit by the enemy it would also give the impression that these non combatants had been kidnapped and forced to print the proclamation under penalty of death. Of course this was not the case as the three tradesmen were union members and sympathetic to the cause. Much of the Proclamation was based on the constitution of the Citizen Army drawn up three years previous and had set out as its first principle that "the ownership was vested of right in the people of Ireland". In it as well was stated "the Republic guaranteed equal rights and equal opportunities to all its citizen's" based, again, on the Citizen Army constitution which stated "equal rights and opportunities for the Irish people", perhaps those who claim some kind of inheritance to the views of James Connolly and actions of the Irish Citizen Army in modern times should act accordingly or stop telling lies or practice what they preach.

The Citizen Army had gone in less than three years from being primarily a picket and freedom of assembly defence force to becoming a revolutionary socialist armed force with a clear and concise political objective. Should the coming rising be a success the political agenda of the Irish Citizen Army was far more reaching than defeating an occupying enemy, the British Crown Forces and establishment, but also the new enemy which would emerge in almost mirror image fashion, native Irish capitalism and this the Citizen Army were in no doubt about.

By about 11.30 a.m. on Monday 24th April 1916 when the bugler, William Oman of the Citizen Army, sounded the fall in about 210 men, women and boys of the same army had mustered. Five minuets later the first section marched off under the command of Captain Richard McCormack to seize Harcourt Street railway station. There then followed a section under Captain Sean Connolly to occupy the City Hall and other buildings commanding Dublin Castle. Another section under Commandant Michael Mallin, Connolly's overall second in command, with Lieutenant Constance Markievicz, Connolly had made her an officer in recognition of women's equality, as his own second in command set out for St. Stephens Green. Perhaps, with the gift of hindsight, Mallins major error during Easter Week was not taking the Shelbourne Hotel which was to hang like a ghostly giant over the Stephens Green Garrison for the duration of the rising, the Irish Citizen Army was soon to be in action leaving behind them a deserted Liberty Hall. It was perhaps symbolic that the first shots of the rising came from the Citizen Army in an attack on the upper Guards Room at Dublin Castle which also brought about the first casualty of Easter Week in the shape of Captain Sean Connolly, Irish Citizen Army, who commanded this section. He was shot by a sniper on the roof of the City Hall and despite the efforts of Dr Kathleen Lynn, subdued to his wounds received from a sniper on the Castle ramparts.]

The assault on the Castle could, and perhaps should, have been one of the most important captures of the rising, though due to the overestimation of the strength enjoyed by the defenders it was never intended to be captured, both in terms of propaganda and tactically. Perhaps not enough homework had been done on the military strength of the defenders who, as it turned out, would have stood little chance against Connolly's troops. It was felt that the Castle could not be taken without a force of hundreds of men and the most Captain Connolly had was twenty. In hindsight this would have been sufficient to take the weakly defended Castle but at the time this was not known. This error was not only to cost the insurgents advantage and position but also Sean Connolly his life. The moral to the story is always do your groundwork and reconnaissance first, no matter how many times or how long it takes. The failure to take Dublin Castle was to prove, along with the equally erroneous move not to take the Shelbourne Hotel on St. Stephens Green, a strategic disaster for the insurgents. In fact the failure to take the Shelbourne was perhaps a nose in front in terms of military mistakes because it allowed the British to place a machine gunner in the hotel which kept Mallin's troops pretty much pinned down until they were forced to retreat to the College of Surgeons. However critical we may be of the failure to occupy these two positions it is with the gift of hindsight, a privilege not enjoyed by those in action at the time. As has been said the numbers the British had in defence of Dublin Castle has turned out to have been vastly overestimated by the Citizen Army and, again with hindsight, it may well have been possible for them to take the Castle with Sean Connolly's force. However at the time it was felt that a force of hundreds would be needed to perfect such a capture so under the perceived conditions, it could well be argued, the main reason for not taking the position was shortage of manpower. The same reason could be sited for not occupying the Shelbourne Hotel, once again shortage of personnel appearing to have been the problem. In the original plans the hotel was to have been occupied but unfortunately 'simply because as a result of MacNeill's countermanding order there were insufficient men available to seize and secure the hotel' (Robbins: P.101).

Eoin MacNeill's countermanding of all manoeuvres for the Irish Volunteers caused much confusion within the republican ranks. As a result of this betrayal the numbers who turned out from that organisation were far fewer than there would have been had the order not been issued. Although the Irish Citizen Army turnout, they were not affected by MacNeill's countermand, was one hundred percent only a minority of the Volunteers answered the call. Constance Markievicz wrote of MacNeill "when Professor Eoin MacNeill and Mr B. Hobson had treacherously acted as cowards part secretly through the IRB, and publicly through the daily papers" she was partly referring to MacNeill's countermanding order published in the papers. This of course depleted the forces on the ground which led to many of the original plans being altered or cancelled the occupation of the Shelbourne was one such casualty. Had Mallin had the gift of hindsight he may well, in all probability, have decided to take the hotel with the personnel he had available had he known the consequences of not doing so.

What was also symbolic was that while the tricolour flew over the GPO Connolly, as only he could, arranged for the Starry Plough, the flag of the Citizen Army to be hoisted over the Imperial Hotel where Jim Larkin had briefly addressed the crowd on bloody Sunday during the Lockout and was the property of none other than William Martin Murphy. In a message Connolly sent with the flag he said, "William Martin Murphy had then triumphed over Labour but that now Labour triumphed over Murphy and his class".

Though the insurgents as a whole tried their best to minimise civilian casualties inevitably, as in any war, there were casualties. One unfortunate incident occurred when some Citizen Army men were trying to construct a barricade using motor cars from a garage showroom. A civilian employee refused to assist in the construction of the obstacle and, because his objections were actively hindering the work, he was shot by some overzealous volunteer.

As history now tells us The Easter Rising, as expected by Connolly who had intimated to a few confides that they were "going out to be slaughtered", ended in defeat for the insurgents at least militarily. However morally it can be reasonably claimed it was not a defeat at all. Given the fact that MacNiell, the leader of the Volunteers, had countermanded all manoeuvres on his hearing of the proposed rising (it is thought a Limerick man, Liam Manahan suspected the plans for a rising and informed MacNiell) coupled with the fact that Sir Roger Casement along with Captain Monteith had been discovered at Banna Strand off the Kerry coast trying to procure weaponry, and resulting in the loss of around 20,000 rifles for the insurrection. Coupled with the fact that the far superior numbers and weaponry on the British side, including the Gunboat *Helga* which sailed up the River Liffey and bombarded Liberty Hall (fortunately empty at the time) and lobbed shells over Dublin as a whole, a moral victory can justifiably be claimed. As the same British Gunboat fired on Liberty Hall for about an hour but failed to score any direct hits. Ironically, and by comparison, Murphy's Citadel, the Imperial Hotel, was obliterated while the fortress of labour remained relatively in tact.

On Saturday 29th April 1916, with the Commandant of all the Irish forces in Dublin James Connolly seriously wounded and the city lying in ruins the overall commander in chief and president of the Irish Republic Padraig Pearse ordered the surrender on behalf of the Irish Volunteers, and Connolly endorsed the same surrender as Commandant of the Citizen Army. This was to save further suffering and damage to the city and its inhabitants. Connolly, who seldom misjudged matters, if what has been recited by many historians is correct, got it wrong when he prophesied that "capital would never destroy capital". This, in the case of Dublin, proved to be a miscalculation. They would destroy capital if they believed it would be cheaper in the long term and would save them any further trouble.

Perhaps the saddest sight that evening of surrender would have been the image of the petit figure of nurse Elizabeth O'Farrell, Cumann na mBan, approaching Brigadier General William Lowe to present the surrender.

When the surrender reached the outlying areas there were optimistic plans, particularly by Michael Mallin, to move through the British lines incognito as civilians and move into the Dublin Wicklow hills. Here, so the theory went, the struggle could be continued using the tactic of guerrilla warfare. However this bold and inventive plan unfortunately never reached fruition and with Connolly lying seriously wounded, as well as him having countersigned the surrender on behalf of the Citizen Army, when the messenger reached Commandant Mallin he decided to obey the order to surrender.

With the surrender complete the insurgents were left in no doubt as to the opinions held by the majority of the citizens of Dublin. The mindless views of some were expressed in such a way that could only exist in the childish imagination of the *"lumpenproletariat"* urging the British forces to reap their revenge on the insurgents in the most barbaric way imaginable. They cheered the British waving Union Jacks and particular slavish praise was reserved for the Staffordshire Regiment as they marched the captured rebel prisoners into Richmond Barracks. Some of the milder opinions held by the mob of what the British should do to the prisoners were suggestions such as "shoot the traitors" and "Bayonet the bastards", cries which rang out emphatically to the young Englishmen of that Regiment. It can only be imagined that if the British had not court-martialled and imprisoned the rebels then the mob would have willingly relieved them of this responsibility and carried out the proceedings for them. On a more positive note it should be remembered that the views of the mob, as only mobs opinions can, changed from the negative to the positive after the executions of the sixteen men.

The composition of the Irish Citizen Army during the Easter Rising covering three theaters was: 'St Stephens Green/Royal College of Surgeons area (118), GPO/Lower O'Connell Street area (47) and the City Hall/Dublin Castle area (43)' (Source: *James Connolly; A Full Life.* Donal Nevin:P733). The officers consisted of James Connolly, Commandant-General, Michael Mallin, Chief of Staff, James O'Neill (later to become Commandant) Quarter Master General. Other officers were Captains: Sean Connolly, Richard McCormack, John O'Neill, William Partridge, Christie Poole. There then followed three Lieutenants; P. Jackson, Michael Kelly and Constance Markievicz followed by Sergeants Joseph Doyle, Madeleine ffrench-Mullen, James Kelly, Seamus McGowan, T.O'Donohue and Frank Robbins.

Twenty seven women of the Citizen Army participated in the rising of which fifteen were in the Stephens Green garrison, ten were stationed in the City Hall/Dublin Castle garrison and two were in the GPO/Imperial Hotel garrison. The Chief Medical Officer of the Irish Citizen Army was Dr. Kathleen Lynn, one of the twenty seven women. The Citizen Army Boys Corps including its O/C, Walter Carpenter (jnr) and Roderick Connolly (son of the Commandant) also participated. The largest number of Citizen Army personnel were concentrated in the Stephens Green area and numbered around 100 approximately half of the total number of Irish Citizen Army volunteers throughout the city. These personnel were under the command of Commandant Michael Mallin and his Lieutenant Constance Markievicz, second in command. During the rising eleven members of the Citizen Army were killed in action these were James McCormack (GPO); Captain Sean Connolly, Louis Byrne, George Geoghegan, Sean O'Reilly and Charlie Darcy (City Hall/Dublin Castle); and John Adams, James Corcoran, Philip Clarke, James Fox and Fred Ryan (St. Stephens Green).

The reader may reasonably ask what was the opinion of Jim larkin, the Irish Citizen Army's first Commandant, at the time in the United States of the events of Easter week. Larkin was disappointed that he was in the United States and not Ireland at the time of the Rising thus denying him the opportunity to participate: 'Though fate denied some of us the opportunity of striking a blow for human freedom, we live in hope that we, too, will be given the opportunity' (Berresford Ellis: P.235). However Frank Robbins disputes this impression which Larkin painted of wishing he had been there. Later after his release in 1916, or very early 1917, Robbins was in the USA and had arranged to meet Larkin in a Hotel. When the former union and army leader finally arrived he was very dismissive of Connolly to the point of insulting his memory. He, Larkin, felt that Connolly had no right to be involved in the insurrection and should have "left it to Pearse and the other poets". This is obviously a contradiction of Berresford Ellis's interpretation of Larkin's feelings but we should, however, remember that Frank Robbins met Larkin face to face so his account is first hand.

The republic proclaimed in 1916 was a Peoples Republic, and the declaration of the republic guaranteed national independence, equal rights and opportunities, religious and civil liberties, the right of the Irish people to the ownership of Ireland and universal suffrage for all citizens, men and women. The Irish Communist Organisation at the time comments: 'But the claim of the 1916 Republic to represent the whole people was something more than a capitalist hypocrisy or a confused use of words. What made it more than that was the presence of Connolly in the leadership of the Republic, and the fact that the class conscious workers were the backbone of the army of the Republic. Connolly and the Citizen Army realised that they were in alliance with property owning classes whose long term interests were different from theirs. They knew that when they spoke of "freedom" these classes did not have the same thing in mind as the working class. For property owners, "freedom" can only mean an increase in private property or a strengthening of the political representation of property. For the workers "freedom" means the abolishing private property, and ending the political representation of property. Connolly and the Citizen Army knew this, and knew that, if the Empire was defeated or withdrew, they would probably find themselves in opposition within the republic to their middle class allies of Easter Monday. They knew this, and they knew that by playing a leading part in the struggle for the independent Peoples Republic they were gaining a very advantageous position from which to resist the effects of their temporary allies to establish the exclusive rule of the bourgeoisie if independence were won, and from which to wage a struggle for full freedom of the working classes by establishing a Socialist republic.

'It is this peculiar disposition of class forces-a strong, organised, armed and class conscious working class joined in alliance with the nationalist property owners against imperialism and in support of the Republic, and represented in the leadership of the movement by a Marxist theorist and organiser- which makes it correct to call the 1916 Republic a Peoples Republic, and justified its claim to be representative of the whole people of Ireland'(*A History of the Irish Working Class*: P. Berresford Ellis: P.235/36).

9

TRIALS AND RETRIBUTION

The Easter Rising was a gallant attempt at "joint action" carried out by the Irish Citizen Army and Irish Volunteers to liberate Ireland from the British crown. It was a frontal and brave assault on the worlds oldest and largest empire, the British domain. James Connolly, Commandant General of the Citizen Army who was to command all Irish forces in Dublin, was under no illusions of the task involved and the probable ultimate outcome. We "are going out to be slaughtered" he privately commented as the Irish Citizen Army and Volunteers left Liberty Hall that April day. This prospect did not deter any within the republican ranks, depleted due to the countermanding order canceling all maneuvers issued the previous day by Eoin MacNeill, nominal chief of the larger Volunteers who was appalled at the thought of a rising when he heard what was about to take place which, never the less, did go ahead albeit on a smaller scale than would have been the case without the countermanding.

The rising despite having many socialists within the ranks of the insurgents, revealed in the contents of the proclamation "We declare the right of the people of Ireland to the ownership of Ireland, and to the unfettered control of Irish destinies to be sovereign and indefeasible" was not in itself a socialist revolution. Had the rising been successful it is likely that the initial period of liberation would have many bourgeois connotations and be a liberal democratic system of governance not dissimilar to the rest of Europe. Indeed eventually this is precisely what happened. Had there been a different result meaning a victory for the insurgents it is highly probable that the Irish Citizen Army would have had to fight against their former comrades if necessary in pursuit of the workers socialist republic, "in the event of victory hold on to your guns" as Connolly had previously stated. It is also possible, though all things considered unlikely, that a victorious Easter Rising could have paved the way for a peaceful transition to socialism with no conflict between the former comrades. The reason for this remote possibility is that although not all the signatories of the proclamation were revolutionary Marxists, only James Connolly warranted this title, they were however critical of certain aspects of the capitalist economic system, hence Pearse's critique above. However given the nature of the capitalist system, and its ability to grant temporary reforms in times of crisis only to reclaim them back at a later date, it is highly unlikely that this latter conciliatory scenario would have become the prevailing political landscape, at least not for any length of time. The contradictions between capital and labour resulting in antagonisms would have inevitably surfaced eventually. However what may add weight to this idyllic peaceful transition to socialism theory are the events which occurred in the months of February and October 1917 in Russia, a bourgeois revolution leading to the Bolshevik takeover though it should be remembered there were many differing circumstances between Ireland and Russia of that time. Even in Russia where the revolution was, for a period, successful the antagonisms between capital and labour surfaced particularly with Kerensky's attempts to crush the workers using Cossack troops.

Even though the Easter Rising was not per se a socialist revolution the picture it painted was more than the crown could tolerate. The British establishment through their chief agent, General Sir John Maxwell, could perceive particularly in the likes of James Connolly and Michael Mallin more than just a bunch of independence seeking radicals. In these two men Maxwell could see a political and class enemy who at all costs would have to go.

After the suppression of the rising by numerically superior British forces with the use of heavy artillery along with shelling from the gunboat *Helga,* whose first target was Liberty Hall, the trials and retribution began in earnest. The British establishment were determined, through the medium of Sir John Maxwell, General

Officer Commanding British forces Ireland, to have their pound of flesh and more. Of all the leaders who were to be sentenced to death James Connolly, Commandant General of the Irish Citizen Army, posed the biggest threat politically, economically and militarily. Connolly whose first time in Ireland was as a British soldier (for economic reasons at the time and he was under age) in the Kings own Liverpool Regiment, which was always considered an Irish regiment and therefore never wholly trusted, was to face a firing squad of that same army. Almost two hundred men and women were court-martialled which, by virtue of the fact that they were court martialled, and not tried as civilians, would suggest they were recognised as soldiers and theoretically, but for the use of DORA, should have been treated as prisoners of war and not executed or sentenced to long terms in civilian prisons. However as in most cases which became a little awkward for the British colonial powers of the time this minor detail was conveniently overlooked.

Of the two hundred or so who were court martialled around ninety were sentenced initially to execution by firing squad which was eventually cut down to a more convenient fifteen. We should briefly examine the anecdotal circumstances that survive to this day in which Eamon de-Valera, an Irish Volunteer officer, escaped the firing squad. Despite the myths and anecdotes which surround the case of de-Valera the sparing of his life was little if anything to do with the never proved theory of him been an American citizen. The chief prosecutor for the crown was a Mr William Wyllie and he recalls having a conversation with the GOC which may, he considers, have determined de-Valera's fate. Maxwell asked him "who was the next on the list for trial" (the term court-martial being conveniently dropped). Wyllie replied "de-Valera Sir". "Never heard of him before", the GOC indicated, to which Wylie responded "he was in command of Bowlands Bakery in the Ringsend area". "I wonder would he be likely to make trouble in the future" continued Maxwell. The prosecution council answered 'I wouldn't think so Sir. I don't think he's important enough. From what I hear he's not one of the leaders' (*From Behind A Closed Door,* Brian Barton P. 76). It was more likely to have been de-Valera's ranking on the barometer of importance which saved his life rather than the unproven American citizen factor. However the USA did make representation on behalf of de-Valera in Dublin on the grounds that he **may** be an American citizen which **may** have been of some help but not the defining factor. It is evident from a report, dated August 1916, by the governor of Dartmoor gaol where de-Valera was being held, that 'neither the authorities nor the prisoner himself knew with certainty his national identity. The report states the prisoner gives New York as his place of birth. He states he has asked his mother to find out whether his father -who was Spanish- became an American citizen. If so, he (prisoner) claims to be such. If not he is Spanish' (Barton P75). There appears to be no documentation of de-Valera's registration as an American citizen and the US authorities were clearly unsure of his nationality and merely stated 'that he was understood to be an American citizen' (ibid). On this evidence it appears more likely that Wylie's valuation of de-Valera's importance was the defining factor in saving his life.

Of the fifteen (sixteen if we include Sir Roger Casement who was hanged in London's Pentonville Gaol) sentenced to death for their part in the rising two were members of the Irish Citizen Army. These were James Connolly, Commandant General, and Michael Mallin, Chief of Staff, who was the officer commanding Stephens Green. Constance Markievicz, also a member of the Citizen Army and Mallin's second in command, was court martialled but escaped the firing squad 'exclusively because of her gender' (Barton P.77). It would not have been the done thing for the British who, for some obscure reason, still considered themselves to be living in the age of chivalry to have murdered a damsel in distress. Constance Markievicz was one of a number of women, along with Helena Maloney, Dr Kathleen Lynn, Marie Perolz, Maeve Cavanagh, Diana Hunter and many others who were imprisoned for their part in the Easter Rising as well as being members of the Irish Citizen Army. This revolutionary socialist army practised equality between the genders both ideologically and in practice and James Connolly's personal assistant, Winifred Carney, was also to bear arms for the Citizen Army during the insurrection.

After the Easter Rising and when the trials and retributions had died down many POWs belonging to both the Citizen Army and Volunteers were interned at the Frongoch internment camp in Wales. Frank Robbins of the Citizen Army, in his statement, outlines the events which took place for him after the Rising.

"Our first introduction to the internment camp was when we were met at the railway station at Bala by some officers of the camp who instructed our guards as to how we should reach our destination. On arriving at the camp we were lined up and handed over to the commandant. There was a Sergeant Major in charge of the camp arrangements who had seen long service in the British Army in many countries and he proceeded along the ranks, questioned each prisoner, and searched him for articles which were prohibited in the camp of which we had none because of our previous rigorous conditions in Knutford Prison. The Sergeant Major, as each batch of prisoners entered the camp, always insisted on looking for "Jackknives", and because of this he was given the nick-name of Jackknife by the prisoners. The Commandant of the prison was nick-named Buckshot because he, like the Sergeant Major, insisted on reminding each batch of prisoners arriving at the camp that all the guards were armed with buckshot and that they were all very good shots, also that they had instructions to shoot any prisoner who would attempt to go near the wires that surrounded the camp".

While interned in Frongoch many incidents occurred, some humorous others less so, which no doubt helped pass the time. "An advisory Committee was set up to investigate every prisoners case, and to recommend to the British Government their decision on each of these cases. The prisoners were taken in batches in alphabetical order from the camp and brought to London, which was a whole days journey. Batches were sent each day, alternatively one batch of prisoners was sent to Wormwood Scrubs Prison and another to Wandsworth Prison. The batch of prisoners in which I was included was sent to the latter prison, and we were each given a separate cell. On our second day at Wandsworth we were brought before the Advisory Committee under the chairmanship of Judge Sankey, who later became Lord Sankey".

"The prisoners were offered a solicitor, named McDonell who had been bought and paid for by Irish men and women who were sympathetic to the cause of liberation and resided in London. The role of the solicitor was to advise the prisoners how they should react and answer questions that would be put by the Advisory Committee". Frank Robbins happened to be in one of the first few of his batch to see the Advisory Committee and he heard the advice which Mr Mcdonell was giving. "My youthful ineptuousness drove me to instruct him and say that we were very thankful to our London-Irish friends, but that I thought it was a waste of effort on his part and a waste of good money on their part to have him there; that as far as we were concerned, we were not retracting in any way from the stance we had taken. This was followed by the remainder of our prisoners and our friend McDonells advice was discarded".

When Frank Robbins entered the room where the Sankey Commission sat the first thing he perceived was a group of men arranged along one side of a large table very official looking. "I was ushered to the opposite side by the attendant and was placed beside a big chair facing Judge Sankey". As far as Frank Robbins can recall in his statement the interview went like this, he continues, "Judge Sankey addressed me by my Christian name, and opened the conversation by saying good-day Frank. Wont you sit down. I did so and thanked him. He then said your name is Frank Robbins?. My answer was yes. Your home address is 39 North William Street Dublin, the answer was yes again. You are a member of the Irish Citizen Army?, he asked. The answer was again in the affirmative. You did not reside in your home address since 24th April, I answered this is not correct. With this reply there was a little rusling and shuffling of papers and I was asked to say when I had last resided at my home address. I gave them the date, Thursday 23rd March. There was a further rustling and shuffling of papers. These straightforward answers seemed to have upset the Advisory

Committee. Judge Sankey then said to me, Frank, you are down here as having the occupation of a driller. Tell us what that means. I replied , that is the designation of my trade in the Dublin Dockyard. I thought it meant that you were drilling holes in soldiers, said Judge Sankey at which there was a general laugh". The last statement by the Judge may give the reader an indication of the contempt the ruling classes and their agents treat their cannon fodder soldiers with, they despise them privately, and publicly uphold them as heroes. Frank Robbins statement continues; "His next question was in the form of a suggestion that I had been forced to take the part in the insurrection against His majesty's Government. I replied that is not so. I entered into the insurrection of my own free will and knowledge of what I was doing. He then suggested that I did not take an active part in the shooting, that I was probably attached to the Red Cross. I told him that I was not so, as I did not know anything about Red Cross work. He then wanted to know if I had fired many shots , my reply to that was that they were uncountable. He then asked, do you think you killed or wounded many soldiers?, to which I replied, I could not say, not being on the other end, this reply was greeted by more general laughter" (Extracts from statement given by Frank Robins member of the Irish Citizen Army1913, Sergeant 1916; subject National Events 1913-1921 including Easter Week Rising 1916. W/S 585, courtesy National Archives). As can be gleaned from Frank Robins statement to the Sankey Commission he was in no way apologetic for his part played in the Easter Rising, to the point of contributing some humour to his answers offered to the Judges questions. He was released in August 1916. The judge also shared some of this humour, the question which must be asked is; what would a member of the British forces on the receiving end of the rebel fire have felt listening to a member of his own ruling class share in the humour offered to the court and, indeed shared by the same court, at his expense? Surely this must highlight the utter contempt shown to the average British Tommy by the ruling classes!

10

THE COURT MARTIAL OF JAMES CONNOLLY

James Connolly was the revolutionary Marxist Commandant General of the Irish Citizen Army who took over from Jim Larkin after his departure for the USA, he was executed by the British on May 12th 1916. He was born at 107 Cowgate Edinburgh, Scotland, on June 5th 1868 of Irish immigrant parentage, though there is some confusion over this location not helped by the fact that completing the 1901 census forms Connolly put his place of birth down as that of his mother, Monaghan. This could have been Connolly trying to emphasize, overemphasize, his Irish pedigree which was frankly inconsistent with his internationalist political position. On the other hand there could well be another perfectly rational explanation for this invention. Connolly, at the time, was reportedly AWOL from the British army and his thinking behind using his mothers place of birth may well have been to muddy the waters sufficiently to throw the authorities off any scent. If this was the case it worked because for Connolly there are no records of him being charged with been absent without leave from the British army. His early political experiences were spent in the Scottish Socialist Federation and the Independent Labour Party in the company of John Leslie, Harold Hydman and the founder of the Independent (later to become the British) Labour Party James Kier Hardy. John Leslie had a liberating affect on Connolly, as did Connolly on him, and because of this he, Connolly, would strive forward with new confidence. His rooms at 21 South College Street became a hive of socialist activity and industry.

Ironically Connolly's first arrival in Ireland was as a young British soldier serving with the Kings Liverpool Regiment, which was known as an Irish regiment, and because of such was never wholly trusted by the Crown. The regiment was stationed in Ireland from 1882 until 1889 and during this period Connolly gained much military know how which, unknowns to him at the time, would come in useful during the years ahead of him. It was economic necessity which had forced Connolly into joining the army and was certainly no love for Queen (Victoria) and country, neither was it anything to do with some far sighted notion of getting weaponry training, although this was to later prove an asset. On his return to Scotland, having gone AWOL from the army, Connolly's financial situation was becoming intolerable. Perhaps the poverty suffered by Connolly and his family at this time in his native Edinburgh can be briefly summed up by describing an occurrence in 1895 when he tried to turn his hand to shoe repairing. This venture in trying to scrape a living together, with most of his customers being fellow socialists, ended after a couple of months when the business collapsed. When Connolly closed the door of his tiny shop for the last time he commented to himself "I'm going out to buy a mirror to watch myself starve to death".

He had a wife Elizabeth who he met while serving as a soldier in Ireland and a family. His friend and comrade, John Leslie, set himself the task of finding Connolly employment within the labour movement. His efforts were rewarded with a response to an appeal placed in the bulletin *Justice*, from Ireland, and was an invitation from the Dublin Socialist Club inviting him to become its paid organizer. This offer Connolly accepted and his wage was to be £1.00 per week, when he could get it or when they could afford to pay him, but this was of little consequence to Connolly who set about the reorganization of the Dublin Socialist Club. Out of this reorganization in 1896 the Irish Socialist Republican Party (ISRP) was born. This new socialist party was to base its ideologies on those of Karl Marx earlier in the 19th century and on Connolly's own experiences with Hydmans Social Democratic Federation back in Scotland. The ISRP also had delegates nominated affiliated to the ill fated Second International which Connolly was to later condemn over the support given by these clandestine class traitors to their native bourgeoisie for the first imperialist war. A condemnation echoed by V.I. Lenin though the pair never met. As if to emphasise the Marxist connection Karl Marx's daughter Eleanor and her husband Edward Aveling became members of the ISRP. The party, under Connolly's stewardship, were involved in a number of political initiatives including opposing the visit of Queen Victoria, christened "the famine Queen" by Maud Gonne, in 1900 and they were heavily involved with organizing the centenary commemoration of the United Irishmen rebellion in 1898.

In 1902 Connolly fought an election in the Wood Quay ward in Dublin, polling 436 votes. Standing on a socialist ticket he was condemned by the priests from the pulpit and any Catholic who voted for him was threatened with excommunication so much was the fear felt by the establishment of Connolly's politics. The publicans reportedly gave away free ale to lure the voters not to elect Connolly and the establishment put it out to the Protestants that Connolly was a Catholic, the Catholics that he was a Protestant and the Jewish community that he was anti-Semitic. So much was the detestation felt by the establishment towards the politics of James Connolly. Drunkenness became rife during the election and only when bestiality was observed in the streets did the authorities clamp down. By this time however the electoral damage required to maintain the status quo had been achieved. Needless to say Connolly was not elected. It should be mentioned that Connolly, in order the Jewish electorate could understand, had his manifesto written in Yiddish as well as English. An initiative which at the time was progressive to say the least, even today it would certainly be unique.

After the Wood Quay election Connolly emigrated to the United States, where he was introduced to Syndicalism as an avenue towards working class emancipation, and did not return until 1910. While in the USA awaiting the arrival of his wife, Lillie, and his family were due to arrive his eldest daughter, Mona, was tragically killed in an accident while doing some ironing.

On his return to Ireland James Connolly once again submerged himself into the socialist cause, a cause which was to become an increasing threat to the state and could well have been a contributing factor in the decision by the Crown to execute him. The failure of the Second Socialist International to oppose the First World War sickened Connolly equally so as it did the Russian revolutionary and signatory to this group V.I. Lenin who went on to lead the Bolshevik revolution in what became Soviet Russia, and also formed the Third International which Connolly would not see. The failure of the Second International to prevent the war was a leading factor which led Connolly to the belief that insurrection was the only practical way to free Ireland and the working class from the yolk of British Imperialism. It was also a firm belief of Connolly's that the working class were ultimately the only truly revolutionary class and the rightful owners of Ireland, *"the cause of labour is the cause of Ireland, the cause of Ireland is the cause of labour they can never be dissevered"*. A revolution led by, and from the working class was always Connolly's first preference of revolutionary struggle and armed conflict waged by a small minority was very much a secondary approach towards achieving the same goal. However once Connolly had realised that such a proletarian insurrection was not to be forthcoming he committed himself to his second preference, even if he and the Citizen Army had to fight alone.

Connolly's reservations about the effectiveness of the rifle and, therefore armed struggle, can be seen in his answer responding to Victor Berger, who was a strong advocate of the rifle. Connolly stated, all be it in the United States at the time, 'The rifle is, of course, a useful weapon under certain circumstances, but these circumstances are little likely to occur. This is an age of complicated machinery in war as in industry, and confronted with machine guns, and artillery which kill at seven miles distance, rifles are not likely to be of much material value in assisting the solution of the labour question in a proletarian manner' (James Connolly: *Collected Works Volume Two* P.243). A few years later these "certain circumstances" were to occur in Ireland. Although Connolly was answering Victor Berger in the USA at the time and was referring to the military might possessed by the capitalist class in that country it must be remembered that Britain also possessed the same weaponry, the weaponry used to steal by force an empire. His conclusion therefore on the use of the rifle could not have been specific to the United States of America, but all advanced capitalist countries (of which the United States was not the power it is today) whose bourgeoisie had much to lose should socialist revolution break out. Connolly's reservations, not to be mistaken with reluctance, about the use of the rifle was to be proved correct with the British using every weapon of "mass destruction" appertaining to the time against the insurgents of Dublin. This equally does not mean there is no place for weaponry and armed struggle in any revolutionary pursuit of proletarian power because ultimately it would be an essential ingredient. It was almost certainly Connolly's private hope that the armed insurrection would have stirred the masses from their slumber and brought about his first preference of freeing Ireland, that been socialist revolution by the working class. Unfortunately this did not occur, much to the disappointment of the Commandant General of the Irish Citizen Army and his troops. Once Connolly had committed himself and the Citizen Army to the idea of a rising it was one hundred per cent commitment from there in even if, which turned out not to be the case, they had to fight alone.

It could be reasonably argued that the politics of James Connolly contributed as much, if not more, than his actions towards the decision to execute him. It could well be said that Connolly's ambitions and actions within the Irish Citizen Army during Easter week provided a form of legitimacy (sic) for the Crown to carry out the execution. The GOC (General Officer Commanding) British forces Ireland, Sir John Maxwell, a so called British officer and gentleman who saw in Connolly somebody who threatened the very existence of his class was determined that James Connolly, Commandant General of the Irish Citizen Army was to stand trial. If we look at some of Connolly's earlier speeches and statements there is little wonder that Maxwell, from his class perspective, was insistent that he, Connolly, must be tried. For example in his earlier days Connolly had drawn no distinction between the national and social questions in Ireland. He maintained that 'the Irish socialist was in reality the best patriot, but in order to convince the Irish people of that fact he must first learn to look inward upon Ireland for his justification, rest his arguments upon the facts of Irish history, and be a champion against the subjection of Ireland and all that it implies' (*The Life and Times of James Connolly*: C. Desmond Greaves P.74). Another quote of Connolly's, again from his ISRP days and, equally which antagonised Maxwell and all he had ever believed in the often quoted, 'If you remove the English army tomorrow and hoist the green flag over Dublin Castle, unless you set about the organization of the socialist republic, your efforts would be in vain. England would still rule you. She would rule you through her capitalists, through her landlords, through her financiers, through the whole array of commercial and industrialist institutions she has planted in this country and watered with the tears of our mothers and the blood of our martyrs. England would still rule you to ruin, even while your lips offered hypocritical homage at the shrine of that freedom whose cause you betrayed' (Greaves: P.85). Further quotes made by James Connolly from earlier times such as *"Socialism represents the dominant and conquering force of our age, the hope of the worker, the terror of the oppressor, the light of the future. Workers of Ireland, salute that light, when once it shines full upon your vision the shackles of ages will fall from your limbs. Freedom will be your birthright."* It was Maxwell's class who had imposed the *"shackles of ages"*. Another statement of Connolly's stated *"When the hour of the social revolution at length strikes and the revolutionary lave now pent-up in the socialist movement finally overflows and submerges the kings and classes who now rule and run the world, high up in the temple of liberty a liberated human race will honour the heroes and martyrs who have watered the tree of liberty, with the blood of their body and the sweat of their intellect"*, (Quotes taken from *James Connolly, a Full Life*: Donal Nevin). For these reasons which had a great impact on the way Maxwell thought, Connolly had to be, not only tried but found guilty and executed, he was not only a military enemy but more importantly a class foe. This was despite Connolly suffering horrendous injuries received during the fighting of Easter week. Maxwell saw in Connolly not only a military opponent but also a class foe and for this reason, if no other, the fate of Connolly was arguably sealed.

During the 1913 Dublin Lockout in the absence of Jim Larkin who was serving a prison sentence Connolly assumed charge of the ITGWU. During this period he also showed the skills of a good negotiator and tactical strategist. Prior to the Askwith Inquiry (chaired by Sir George Askwith) into the events of the lockout Connolly spoke, for the union, a more conciliatory note. Connolly implied that the union was prepared and willing to let things remain as they were, those been the forces of capital and labour remaining in a state of what he termed "armed neutrality". He then began speaking of a "fight to the finish" as more oratory than reality. Connolly perceived "no fight is ever really fought to the finish" adding a word of caution to the employers as well as the olive branch. "Of course if the employers persist in fighting this way, we are perfectly ready to do so", in other words if they wish to continue down this avenue then so are we. This was Connolly at his tactical best. Knowing the class make up of the Askwith Inquiry would not be wholly impartial therefore if the union were seen to be giving a little ground, albeit orally, it would make it easier for any sympathetic persons sitting on the inquiry to lean the unions way. If the ITGWU were seen to have given a little and the employers were still entrenched in their intransigent positions it could be seen as good will on behalf of the union without giving up one demand. This shrewdness shown by Connolly was no doubt nearly three years later noticed by General Maxwell. This would be perceived as a further sign of danger as Connolly had shown an ability to woe the liberal elements sitting on the Askwith Inquiry while still remaining a danger. Therefore this was an opportunity to get rid of him once and for all!

It could be stated, with reasonable justification, that had Connolly and the Citizen Army not been involved in the rising, with their anti-capitalist ideology and socialist ambitions, then there could have been a remote possibility that the executions which took place may have been commuted to long terms of imprisonment. Whereas the Citizen Army was opposed to the economic system of capitalism based on the exploitation of the many by the few, within the ranks of the Irish Volunteers such ideology where it did exist was not the primary source of discontent. The chief prosecutor, William Wylie, recalls a conversation he had with the GOC during which Maxwell asked 'who is next on the list?' (*From Behind A Closed Door*: Brian Barton P.291) to which Wylie replied "Connolly Sir" and Maxwell's response was definite. 'Well I must insist on him being tried' (ibid), Maxwell bawled, much to Wylie's discomfort who pointed out that the prisoner was seriously wounded. This cut no ice with the leader of British Imperialism in Ireland who replied with much insistence and indicating the irrelevance of Connolly's condition the court can be convened in hospital. Wylie again voiced his concern about Connolly's fitness to stand trial but so much was Maxwell's determination that his class enemy would cause him no more turbulence by standing trial, and a guilty verdict arrived at that he ignored Wylie. The documents presented by the prosecution during the trial were marked X and Y, with Connolly's defense which he desired be given to his wife marked Z. The charge read '1) Did an act to wit did take part in an armed rebellion and in the waging of war against His Majesty the King, such act o such a nature as to be calculated to be prejudicial to the Defence to the Realm with the intention and for the purpose of assisting an enemy. 2) Did attempt to cause disaffection among the civilian population of His Majesty' (*From Behind a Closed Door*: Brian Barton P.295). Connolly's defense was in sharp contrast to that of Michael Mallin, his Chief of Staff as we shall see. Connolly insisted that his defense document be lettered Z and read as follows 'I do not wish to make any defense against charges of wanton cruelty to prisoners. These trifling allegations that have been made in that direction if they record facts that really happened deal with the almost unavoidable incidents of a hurried uprising, and overthrowing of long established authorities, and nowhere show evidence of a set purpose to wantonly injure unarmed prisoners.

We went out to break the connection between this country and the British Empire and to establish an Irish Republic. We believe that the call we thus issued to the people of Ireland was a nobler call in a holier cause that (sic) any call issued to them during this war having any connections with the war.

We succeeded in proving that Irishmen are ready to die endeavoring to win for Ireland their national rights which the British Government has been asking them to die to win for Belgium. As long as that remains the case the cause of Irish freedom is safe. Believing that the British Government has no right in Ireland, never had any right, the presence in any one generation of even a respectable minority of Irishmen ready to die to affirm that truth makes that government for ever a usurpation and a crime against human progress.

Personally thank God that I have lived to see the day when thousands of Irishmen and boys, and hundreds of Irish women and girls, were equally ready to affirm that truth and seal it with their lives if necessary' (Barton: P.298). As can be drawn by the reader from that statement written on document Z Connolly was unrepentant and had no regrets for his actions. The next Wylie heard of the episode was that Connolly had been tried and condemned, found guilty on charge one and not guilty on the second less serious charge, he had no idea who the prosecutor was. So much was the GOC Ireland's determination to have Connolly court martialled as early as possible that the whole scene took place in a hospital ward with the prisoner propped up in his bed. James Connolly was executed strapped to a chair in the yard of Kilmainham Gaol on May12 1916.

11

THE COURT MARTIAL OF MICHAEL MALLIN

In 1916 Michael Mallin was aged 42. He was of small, slight appearance with a long curving moustache with thick dark hair. Mallin was, by trade, a silk weaver and in the course of plying his trade he was also an organiser of labour, he was a devout catholic and a member of the Working Men's Temperance Committee. He was Secretary of the Silk Weavers Union before joining the Irish Transport and General Workers Union after its formation by Jim Larkin. From around 1909 and for a period thereafter he owned a shop which, due to the poverty which existed during the 1913 Dublin Lockout, had been forced to close. As a member of the Irish Transport and General Workers Union Michael Mallin was active within that organisation on many fronts. For example he was a band instructor for the union and took this role as serious as any of his other duties within the union. Put plainly he was dedicated to the cause and victory of organised labour over capitalism.

Like his Commandant General of the Irish Citizen Army, James Connolly, Michael Mallin was an ex British serviceman who, again like Connolly, had enlisted in 1888 for purely economic reasons and not for any love of Queen and/or country. Mallin did love his country, Ireland, in a much more progressive way a way which he would pay the ultimate sacrifice that being his life. Michael Mallin was only fourteen when he enlisted in the British army and the most formative years of his political development appears to have come from his experiences in the service of the crown, in the Royal Fusiliers. 'Over the next twelve years he saw service in India and then in South Africa and it was there he acquired strong pro-Boer and anti-imperialist sympathies' (*From Behind A Closed Door*, Brian Barton P268). Like his

Commandant there is no truth in the romantic notion that Mallin joined the British army for weaponry training, this is a myth which has grown around both men in certain romantic minority circles over the years. Before the First World War Mallins home had been in Inchicore on Dublin's South side. He joined the Irish Citizen Army at its inception in November 1913, 'becoming its Chief of Staff when Connolly became its Commandant in 1914' (ibid) after Jim Larkin's departure for the USA. Part of Mallins duties as second in command only to Connolly was to organise indoor exercises, scouting, manoeuvres and signalling, along with many other military associated tasks and duties. Mallin was very keen on drilling and was enthusiastic to learn more about military strategy and organisation. 'He was particularly active in acquiring arms for the force; he was said to have a genius for coaxing weapons from soldiers' (ibid), a gift which was to prove very useful indeed in the not so distant future. Mallins ability to procure weaponry, along with the new uniforms finished off with green slouched hats, made the Irish Citizen Army look exactly that, an army.

Michael Mallin was like his Commandant James Connolly a non drinker and a committed socialist which was probably one of the reasons which prompted Connolly to promote him to Chief Of Staff, though Connolly was not of the same egg when it came to religion. Connolly though a Catholic could never be described as "devout" or even practicing and had many fiery critical arguments with the church. Many present day socialists will argue that a person can not be a devout Catholic and a committed socialist this, like many other subjects along similar lines, is open to interpretation. For reasons of risking causing offense I shall keep my own views exactly that, my own. Mallin showed many of the characteristics and trade marks of Connolly but it could be argued that his defence speech at his trial let him down a great deal, and bore no resemblance to the defence oration, aforementioned by James Connolly. Given the courage which Mallin had shown on the battlefield his defence speech may appear very much out of character and disappointing.

On the battlefield he had rescued men who were under heavy machine gun fire pinned down in St. Stephens Green. He had personally faced these same machine guns without hesitation in order to bring men to safety, therefore the thought of death appeared to hold no fears for Michael Mallin.

The charges against Michael Mallin were as follows 1) 'Did an act to wit did take part in an armed rebellion and in the waging of war against His Majesty the King, such an act being o such a nature (sic) as to be calculated to be prejudicial to the Defence of the Realm and being done with the intention and for the purpose of assisting the enemy'.

2) 'Did attempt to cause disaffection among the civilian population of His Majesty' (*From Behind a Closed Door*: Brian Barton P.276). The charges aimed at Mallin were worded exactly the same as those of which Connolly was charged with and the verdict exactly the same, guilty death, first charge not guilty second charge. It could be argued that as Mallin was tried four days before Connolly that he had nothing to base his defence speech on. However his oration in his defence does raise certain questions of Michael Mallin under severe pressure.

Defence Statement.

'I am a silk weaver by trade and have been employed by the Transport Union as band instructor. During my instruction of these bands they became part of the Citizen Army and from this I was asked to become a drill instructor. I had no commission whatever in the Citizen Army. I was never taken into the confidence of James Connolly. I was under the impression we were going out for manoeuvres on Sunday but something altered the arrangements and the manoeuvres were postponed till Monday. I had verbal instructions from James Connolly to take 36 men to St. Stephens Green and to report to the Volunteer officer there. Shortly after my arrival at St. Stephens Green the firing started and the Countess of Markievicz ordered me to take command of the men as I had been so long associated with them. I felt I could not leave them and from that time I joined the rebellion. I made it my business to save all officers and civilians who were brought into Stephens Green. I gave explicit orders to the men to make no offensive movements and I prevented them attacking the Shelbourne Hotel' (Barton: P. 278).

Firstly as Connolly's chief of staff to say that he "was never into the confidence of James Connolly" is bordering on ludicrous and secondly to state that he "prevented the men from attacking the Shelbourne Hotel" was equally untrue. The reason the Shelbourne was not attacked was a military decision, based on the number of men available reduced due to MacNeill's countermanding, taken by Mallin and his troops and also one of the biggest mistakes of the entire rising as the hotel should in hindsight still have been taken. However these are not the main reasons for criticising Mallins defence speech. The most critical aspect is where he tried to make out and push the blame onto Constance Markievicz by implying that she was in command. She was in fact his second in command and was answerable to him and not the way Mallin suggested at his court martial, which appeared to imply he was answerable to her. He may have been working on the theory that the British would not execute a woman but if this was the case he, Mallin, was playing a very dangerous game with somebody else's life in an attempt to save his own. Nobody could blame Michael Mallin for trying to escape the firing squad after all he had four children and his wife was expecting another child. For this reason escaping the death penalty would have been Mallins priority, however it is the methods adopted in this attempt which raises questions. Maybe the pressure of his court martial coupled with concern for his family caused Michael Mallin to act out of character. Considering his record on the battlefield history should be kind to him as the courageous acts he performed certainly outweigh any digressions. He would have perhaps said anything to survive considering only his wife and family, for this he should not be criminalized as most men would probably have taken a similar line. Michael Mallin was executed on the 8th May 1916 between the hours 3.45 and 4.05am.

12

CONSTANCE (COUNTESS) MARKIEVICZ

No descriptive piece of work on the Irish Citizen Army would be complete without a section on Constance Markievicz, nee Gore-Booth. She was born in London at Buckingham Gate on the 4th February 1868 (Ironically the same year as her future mentor James Connolly came into the world). She was the eldest child of Sir Henry Gore-Booth, heir of Sir Robert Gore-Booth of Lissadell, County Sligo on the West of Ireland. She was born into wealth and privilege and was hardly a candidate for future membership of the Irish Citizen Army. Her family, the Gore-Booths, were a stronghold of the Anglo-Irish world, she was a child of the Protestant Ascendancy. Her title Countess was by virtue of the fact that she was married to a Polish Count, Casmir Markievicz in line with her own class status of the time.

'At Lissadell in the 1860s the tall tree of the Protestant Ascendancy still stood firm as ever in the minds of the Gore-Booths' (*The Rebel Countess*: Anne Marreco P.3). The Liberal Prime Minister William Ewart Gladstone and his talk of Home Rule for Ireland seemed a million miles away, and all his hot air on this subject did not over concern the Gore-Booths. The only but crucial difference between the Gore-Booths, and families like them, and the landed gentry in England was that the position they held was literally that, held, and not freely given. This is not to suggest that landed gentry of any nationality or location should be condoned it was, however, accepted reluctantly in some cases freely by others as the way things were which was not so much the case in Ireland. 'Their forebears had come adventurously and taken possession of conquered lands' (ibid). Though the Gore-Booths were generally regarded, by the standards of the time, as good landlords they continued to be regarded as colonists by the local population they were foreign land grabbers. Constance however was destined to be different, very different.

There were many chapters in the life of Constance Markievicz, which would be too voluminous to print here. For this reason we must skip a few decades to a time more relevant to our subject.

In March 1909 Constance happened to read a newspaper article on the subject of the formation of Boys Brigades and Boy Scouts by the Viceroy. These brigades and troops were reviewed at Clontarf, North Dublin, by the Lord Lieutenant. The thought of this made the Republican blood which by now flowed through Constance's veins boil. She was to write a letter in the *Fianna Magazine*: 'surely nothing sadder could be seen than the sons of men who had thrown in their lot with the Fenians, whose forebears had been out in 48, suffered with Emmet, taken the word of command from Tone, cheered when Sarsfield, or Owen Roe O'Neill led them to victory-nothing could be sadder than to see these boys saluting the flag that flew in triumph over every defeat their nation has known, and from that day it was planted in their country stood for murder, pillage, injustice and treachery' (Marreco: P.112-113). Constance immediately started to plan what to do about the Viceroys scouts . As it happened help lay near at hand in the form of a friend, Bulmer Hobson, in Belfast. He had been making use of some huts used to house British soldiers during the Belfast riots. Bulmer Hobson formed classes of boys and girls for the study of the Irish language, and Irish history; he also encouraged the Gaelic game of hurling by forming a junior Gaelic league. He decided to christen his organisation *Na Fianna Eireann*, after the hero army of ancient Ireland. Constance decided to promote this idea on a broader front as the Belfast experiment lapsed starting in Dublin. Constance's idea was to 'weld the youth of Ireland together to work and fight for Ireland... An organisation that would be broad enough, through love of country, to include all workers for Ireland, in whatever camp they might be... All that would count in the end is their willingness to undertake a life of self-sacrifice and self-denial for their countries sake' (Marrecco: p.113). Her early enthusiasm had not yet addressed the class question hence the statement "whatever camp they might be". The year 1909 is generally regarded as the year *Na Fianna Eireann* was born, formed by Bulmer Hobson and Constance Markievicz. However it is Constance who must take most of the credit for taking the *Fianna* much further and better organised than Bulmer Hobson had in Belfast. *Na Fianna Eireann* were to become the Republican Scouts.

In 1913 Constance became heavily involved on the side and within the ranks of the Irish Transport and General Workers Union and also became a strong admirer of James Connolly and his policies linking the social, economic and national questions into one. She was one of the early volunteers to the Irish Citizen Army and was a member of the first Army Council. During the 1913-14 Dublin Lockout, the womb which gave birth to the Citizen Army, it was not unusual to find Constance in the soup kitchen at Liberty Hall with her sleeves rolled up dishing out soup and bread to the locked out workers and their families. When the lockout came to an end in 1914, with the workers starved back to work, the head of the Employers Federation (forerunner to today's IBEC) William Martin Murphy had failed in his quest to destroy the ITGWU. The union was weakened but not defeated. Murphy's intentions were to defeat and eradicate what he saw as the menace of "Larkinism"

The next momentous event was to be Easter week 1916, which we have already discussed and Constance was appointed second in command at St. Stephens Green to Chief of Staff Michael Mallin, Irish Citizen Army, Mallin been answerable only to James Connolly. When their task of holding the Green became hopeless, due to superior enemy numbers and weaponry, Mallin and Markievicz decided that the Citizen Army should retreat to the College of Surgeons. On Saturday 29th April Padraic Pearse, as Commander in Chief of the Irish Volunteers issued the surrender, which was endorsed by James Connolly as Commandant General of the Irish Citizen Army. When the news reached the College of Surgeons the following day, Sunday, there was a mixture of excitement and anger. Constance moved amongst the insurgents reassuring them and saying "I trust Connolly".

The arresting officer from the British side was a Captain de Courcy Wheeler who, by some twist of fate, was distantly related to Constance as he was married to a kinswoman of the Gore-Booths. Captain Wheeler would give evidence against James Connolly and Michael Mallin as well as Constance at their court-martials. He came to the College of Surgeons on Sunday 30th April to receive the surrender from the insurgents Commander Michael Mallin. 'He met Michael Mallin and Constance at the side-door and had a meeting with them under the flag of truce. Constance handed over her pistol and her Sam Browne belt' (Marreco: P.207). According to Captain Wheeler she kissed the weapon before handing it over. This then was the formal surrender of the Irish Citizen Army at the College of Surgeons, formerly of the St. Stephens Green garrison.. 'Captain de Courcy Wheeler offered to drive Constance by car to the Castle, but she refused, saying she preferred to march with her men , since she was second in command' (ibid). The rebels were taken to Dublin Castle and then to Richmond Barracks and later to Kilmainham Gaol, where they were crowded eight to a cell. Shortly afterwards Constance was isolated and her comrades feared for her life she would, however it is said, have "welcomed death".

At her court martial the charges against her were word for word the same as those which were levelled at Connolly and Mallin however, unlike her Commandant and Chief of Staff who were both found guilty of the first charge but not guilty of the second, less serious offence, she was found guilty on both counts and sentenced to death. The sentence was however commuted to life imprisonment almost certainly on the grounds of her sex. It is broadly reported that Constance would have "preferred death" alongside her comrades from the Citizen Army, and judging by her nature it would be a brave historian who would doubt the reports. Many reasons have been suggested for this reprieve, the most likely as has been mentioned her gender, however according to Esther Roper, a friend of Constance's 'in her opinion it was Asquith's (Prime Minister Herbert Asquith not to be mistaken with Sir George Askwith mentioned earlier) personal intervention that saved Constance's life' (Marreco:P. 210). Herbert Asquith was the British Prime Minister at the time and perhaps the Gore Booth's may have held some influence on his opinions. However this is a possible observation and not a statement of fact and the more probable reason for her reprieve would have been her gender.

While in Kilmainham Gaol Constance made it be known that she wished to convert from the religion of her birth, Protestant, to Roman Catholicism. This was at the time when she thought the firing squad awaited her, before her reprieve, she wished to feel closer to her comrades in death by a "baptism of desire". As we know the death penalty handed down to her was commuted to life imprisonment and as a result she was moved to Mountjoy Gaol. On arriving at this place she immediately began receiving instruction in Catholicism from the Chaplain, the Reverend Father McMahon, 'although she was not in fact received into the Roman Catholic Church until her release from Aylesbury Jail in 1917. This was because, so she said, she did not want to have a religious ceremony in prison' (Marreco: P. 216).

Constance was moved from Mountjoy to Aylesbury Gaol around June 1916 as convict number twelve. She prepared herself for almost any eventuality in Aylesbury but there was one thing however which she was not prepared for and almost drove her insane. 'This was a carved and painted eye in the centre of every cell door, realistic to the last detail, pupil, eye lashes, eyebrow - and provided with a sliding disc on the outside, so authority could substitute its real eye for the artificial one. If a prisoner defaced the eye or covered it she was punished' (Marreco: P. 220). In Aylesbury once she was locked up for the night the only company she had was the ever present eye, not even a pencil and paper to help pass the boredom. This was until her sister, Eva, through constant badgering of the Home Office who finally relented (family pressure perhaps?) and allowed her pencil and paper for drawing. Constance was released from Aylesbury on the 17th June 1917 and was met by a welcome party consisting of her sister, Eva, and Esther Roper, Helena Molony, Marie Perolz and Dr Kathleen Lynn. Another event which tragically occurred during 1917 was the death of another Republican prisoner, Thomas Ashe. He had been imprisoned in August for making seditious speeches. His funeral was, apart from the paying of respects, to be a public demonstration and act of defiance against the authorities. Thomas Ashe died in September of cold, hunger strike and forcible feeding. Among the mourners were the now proscribed uniforms of the Irish Volunteers and the Irish Citizen Army, including Constance in her Citizen Army uniform raising a loud cheer from the crowd. A far cry from the baying mob described above by Frank Robbins outside Richmond Barracks.

In April 1918 the British Government introduced a Bill which, if passed, would empower them to introduce conscription into Ireland. The Bill was, as expected, passed on April 16th even though the Irish Parliamentary Party voted against it to a man. The British Government in order to sweeten the bitter pill, at the same time proposed to introduce a Home Rule Bill. The whole of nationalist Ireland were opposed to conscription and anti conscription meetings took place all over the country. A twenty four hour strike was called bringing the whole country, with the exception of Belfast, to a standstill. The British Army were desperate for cannon fodder and Field-Marshal Lord French was appointed Viceroy and was clear about his task. "Home rule will be offered and declined", he commented to Lord Riddell, "then conscription will be enforced. If they will leave me alone I can do what is necessary". French's plan was to notify a date before which men of fighting age and ability must offer themselves in the various districts, a similar process to that adopted by the Romans during their 400 year occupation of Celtic Britain for their forced labour scheme, failure to do so meant that the authorities would send out the troops to collect the unwilling sacrificial lamb. 'The-Field marshal, for all his despotism, was quite unable to control his sister, Mrs Despard, a militant feminist and republican who vociferously stated her case in the Dublin streets during his tenure of office' (Marreco: P. 239).

French was eager to display his zeal and wasted no time when in April a shipwrecked man was rescued off the coast of Galway by police who he told was a member of Roger Casements illegal Irish Brigade. French immediately concluded that there was a German plot and proceeded to round up the leaders of the *Sinn Fein* party, including Constance. With these people out of the way it would make the road to conscription smoother, an army with no leadership so to speak, or so the authorities thought. Constance Markievicz was to begin a second stint behind bars for her political stance, however this time she was not isolated, her companions were her friends instead of the depraved and desperate inmates of Aylesbury. It was also fortunate for her that she was used to prison life because although she was with like minded company at first this was to change when her two comrades, Maude Gonne and Mrs Clarke (widow of the executed 1916 leader Thomas Clarke) were released leaving her once again alone in a British gaol. In October of 1918 Constance was given the freedom of the city of Limerick as a popular protest against imprisonment while still in captivity. A similar strategy was used by *Sinn Fein* in the by election of 1981 nominating IRA hunger striker Bobby Sands as a candidate to the Westminster parliament.

In November 1918 the British Government called a General Election and *Sinn Fein* decided to contest them. This was a tactical move by the party because they entered on an abstention ticket, meaning that any of their candidates elected would not take their place in the Westminster Parliament. Constance was to stand as a *Sinn Fein* candidate, and her name was submitted for the Dublin St. Patrick's division. She sent out the following election address from Gaol, 'It is with great pleasure that I have been accepted as SF candidate for St. Patrick's constituency. As I will not procure my freedom by giving any pledge or undertaking to the enemy, you will probably have to fight without me. I have many friends in the constituency who will work all the harder for me. They know that I stand for the Irish Republic, to establish which our heroes died, and that my colleagues are firm in the belief that the freeing of Ireland is in the hands of the Irish people today...There are many roads to freedom, today we hope that our road to freedom will be a peaceful and bloodless one; I need hardly assure you that it will be an honourable one. I would never take an oath of allegiance to the power I meant to overthrow. The one thing to bear in mind is that this election must voice the people of Ireland's demand to be heard at the peace conference... we are quite cheerful and ready for anything that comes, ready to stick on here, certain that things are going on just as well without us, and that our voices are even louder than free men's' (Marreco: P. 241).

It was, among many other things, this election which put Constance Markievicz into the history books. *Sinn Fein* won 73 out of 105 seats for Ireland, thanks in many ways to French and his conscription earlier in the year, of which Constance was one. She thus became the first woman in history to be elected to the Westminster Parliament, albeit on an abstention ticket. After this electoral success *Sinn Fein* formed their own Parliament, Dail Eireann (Assembly of Ireland), which the 26 Unionists and 6 non-republican nationalists did not attend. However these were a minority and *Sinn Fein* conducted the affairs of the country albeit illegally in the eyes of the Crown, in what has become known as the "First Dail", which Constance was appointed the Minister for Labour. The "democratic programme" of the first Dail has never been fully enacted and the inconvenient points, most of the programme, conveniently forgotten by today's politicians and governments in Ireland.

While still in Holloway Gaol where she was now involuntarily residing in early 1919 Constance received a letter summonsing her to attend the new Parliament on 11th February. On her release from prison, and as we are now acquainted it was *Sinn Fein* policy to abstain from taking seats in the British Parliament, Constance stayed at Eva's in London. She did visit the House of Commons incognito to see the cloakroom peg with her name on it, the sole outward testament in Britain to her election victory. In march 1919 she returned to Ireland to a reception which a Monarch or President might envy. *The Red Flag* was sang along with *Amhran na bhfiann*, the streets were jammed with the Citizen Army and Irish Volunteers on parade. Constance was however to spend a third spell of incarceration, this time for her supposed visit to a town where she was forbidden by the authorities.

'On Saturday 17th May , Constance came to Mallow on her way to Newmarket- the town forbidden to her by the British authorities- and was met by jubilant crowds who had feared the dauntless Countess might fail them. It was decided to get round the Proscription by holding the meeting that night instead of Sunday as arranged. In her speech she repeated Swifts cry, "Burn everything British but its coal" to the usual enthusiastic applause' (Marreco: P. 246). However once the meeting drew to a close the same problem remained, how to avoid getting arrested the following morning, since the authorities had saturated the town with RIC men and soldiers. 'A plan was devised whereby a brave young lady undertook to masquerade as Constance for that night. At a pre-arranged rendezvous the girl, Miss Madge McCarthy, dressed herself in Constance's clothes and proceeded very openly to the local hotel which was being closely watched by the RIC' (ibid). In the meantime while Miss McCarthy spent the night at the hotel, Constance, dressed as a man, was driven through the RIC patrols and spent the night at Drominorigle. When the embarrassment of this deceit finally dawned on the authorities Constance was eventually arrested. She denied ever been in the hotel, which was perfectly true, but the testimony of the RIC and military that they had seen her address a meeting and then enter the hotel was enough to secure her conviction. She was sentenced to four months imprisonment, this time in Cork Gaol. When she was released from custody the movements of Constance were very shady and sightings patchy, apart from the fact that she never missed a

Dail meeting except when she was in prison. In November 1919 the authorities at Dublin Castle tried to get her deported on the grounds that she was an alien. This futile effort was, of course, even by Castle standards unsuccessful.

1919 was the year which the War of Independence began which the Irish Citizen Army, as a body took little part in more on this below. However individuals and groups of Citizen Army volunteers did take an active role, including Constance. This war was to continue until the signing of the peace treaty with Britain on December 6th 1921. The treaty was accepted by the Irish delegation of Michael Collins, Arthur Griffiths, Robert Barton, Gavan Duffy and Eamon Duggan with Erskine Childers as secretary. The Treaty gave dominion status to 26 of Irelands 32 counties, the six North Eastern counties of the nine county Province of Ulster to remain under British rule. Dominion status for the 26 counties meant that Southern Ireland could elect her own government, raise her own defence force, make her own laws and policies, providing these were not antagonistic towards Britain. This was a far cry from the republican ideal because the government still had to swear an oath of allegiance to the British Monarch, or perhaps more importantly to the "Irish Free State", *Saorstat Eireann,* which in turn swore the allegiance, and the Royal Navy would retain the use of the ports. These ports would become known as "the Treaty Ports". The Treaty would split the republican forces into two increasingly hostile camps, the Pro and Anti-Treaty factions of the Irish Republican Army. The treaty was accepted in the Dail by sixty four votes in favour to fifty seven against. It also split the IRAs 19 divisions with only eight coming out in favour leaving a majority of eleven against. The main sticking point for many of the Anti-Treaty side was the maintenance of the oath of allegiance to the British monarch, as well as an objection to partition. The Women's Council rejected the Treaty by 419 votes against to 63 in favour. Supporters of the Treaty were asked to resign from the Council. The Irish Citizen Army were, as a body, against the Treaty but, similarly again as a body they had taken little part in the War of Independence they had little say. However the individuals and groups of Citizen Army personnel, including Constance, and who had been under the command of the overall Dublin Commander of Republican forces, Oscar Traynor, were of the Anti-Treaty persuasion. On January 10th 1922 Constance ceased to be Minister of Labour, and on the 16th January the new government of the 26 counties moved into Dublin Castle. A terrible Civil War was to ensue.

Throughout the 1920s Constance was always on the move attending meetings and making speeches but slowly the life of a revolutionary was catching up with her. The non-stop activity dating back to before the 1913-14 Dublin Lockout through to Easter Week to her terms of imprisonment and as a consequence neglect were beginning to take their toll. In December 1925 Constance resigned her position as president of *Cumann na mBan,* this was chiefly due to her support for Eamon De Valera and his new *Fianna Fail* party, causing *Sinn Fein* to split. In June 1926 she received the bitter blow of the death of her sister Eva. Constance was to live just over another year herself. There was still another election to fight . Constance undertook the campaign with her usual energy, although there were those among her friends who feared for her health. She broke her arm cranking up her old Ford. She was attended to by a Doctor to whom she declared her intention of going on with her political meeting, "It's lucky its my arm, I can still talk". Constance was adamant she would never take the oath, "how could I meet Jim Connolly and Paddy Pearse in the hereafter if I did she argued". She was re-elected without taking any oath. 'She walked with De-Valera and the other Republican Deputies in an attempt to enter the Dail without taking the oath. But there was little time left now' (Marreco: P.298).

At the end of June Constance was ordered into hospital by Dr Kathleen Lynn because she was so ill. She was operated on for appendicitis. After, what appeared to be, a brief spell of recovery she relapsed and on July 8th she underwent a second operation and developed peritonitis (a condition which causes severe abdominal pain.) On 15th July1927 Constance Markivievicz died age 59. From her birth into riches and privilege, which she rejected, to her involvement and massive contribution to the Dublin poor during the 1913-14 lockout, to being one of the founders of the Irish Citizen Army and right through to her death in 1927 her commitment to the socialist republic never faltered. She died five days before one of her political opponents, Kevin O'Higgins,who was shot dead on his way to Mass by the IRA.

Her body lay in state at the Rotunda, having been refused the use of the City Hall or the Mansion House by the Free State authorities, her funeral procession was huge. 'Thousands lined the streets; the official organisations marched: *Sinn Fein, Fianna Eireann, Inghinidhe na bEireann, Cumann na mBan, Fianna Fail,* ITGWU, Irish Citizen Army. At Glasnevin her Irish Citizen Army uniform was lowered into her grave' (Marreco: P. 300). Free State soldiers were present armed and ready to prevent a volley of shots being fired over her grave. It is often thought by some that Constance died in poverty but this may not be strictly true as some reports say that her sister, Eva who died a year earlier, left her £4,000. If this is the case she still died a lot poorer than she would have done had she not left the life of her birth, but better off than the working classes of Ireland whose cause she championed, and if it is not the case and she did die in absolute poverty, which is unlikely, it is again a tribute to the woman who gave up so much to help so many. One thing is certain and that is despite Constance's shift in political party membership she never left the Citizen Army as her burial testifies. Her old friend from Mountjoy, Father Ryan; the Priest who had began overseeing her conversion to the Roman Catholic faith, was present, faithful to his word to be with her at the end. Nobody could argue that Constance (Countess) Markievicz, nee Gore Booth, had lived a very chequered life and undergone a complete metamorphosis between the cradle and grave.

13

AFTER THE DUST HAD SETTLED
AND THE LABOUR MOVEMENT

After the rising and the dust had settled with the trials and retribution over, prisoners released from various camps and prisons, Ireland would never politically be the same again. With the executions carried out by order of the British GOC, Sir John Maxwell, public opinion formerly, generally speaking, against the rebels had swung in the opposite direction behind the insurgents. It has often been remarked that the British, and in particular John Maxwell, did more to give the rising, albeit belatedly, and the cause of Irish independence more credibility than almost any other factor. It was the policy of the British establishment to have the leaders, and some who were not in positions of leadership, executed which outraged the Irish public, an outrage which legitimised the rising in the general election of November 1918 which saw 73 Sinn Fein candidates returned for the 105 seats for Ireland with its avowed principle of making British rule in Ireland impossible, and now had a mandate to do so. The executions of the leaders of the Easter rising along with the intransigent Lord French's insistence on introducing conscription into Ireland were massive factors contributing to the electoral success of Sinn Fein. Had the same British establishment not executed these men (16 altogether if Sir Roger Casement who was hanged in Pentonville Gaol is included) and sentenced them to long terms of imprisonment, then, under such circumstances it is **possible** that such a change of direction from the Irish public **may** not have been so forthcoming.

As we are aware James Connolly, Commandant General of the Irish Citizen Army and Secretary of the Irish Transport and General Workers Union, was one of those men executed by the British, an ardent Marxist, the ideology which was to follow him to the grave. There are those misguided historians who argue that Connolly's participation in the Easter Rising was a move away from socialism in favour of nationalism, however nothing could be further from the truth as previously outlined. It should be remembered that there were other executed leaders whose political thinking was leftwards leaning to say the least. 'Pearse, MacDonagh, Ceannt, and Clarke were to the left of the Volunteer movement, Pearse challenging the concept of private property and accepting many of Connolly's teachings' (Berresford Ellis: P.236). There were others in the civil provisional government, which was not active during the Easter Rising, who were also to the left in their thinking such as William O'Brien, a Marxist disciple of James Connolly (but this is where the similarity stops because O'Brien may have been a disciple of Connolly's in theory but the practice appears to be somewhat different for more on this issue read *James Larkin: Lion of the Fold*: Chpt. 50 Donal Nevin ed.), along with Tom Kelly and Mrs Sheehy-Skeffington who were both socialists. 'With such representation of the left it would seem that, had 1916 achieved success, a social-democratic system of government would have been the first step in an independent Ireland' (ibid). This assessment by Peter Berresford Ellis would not be dissimilar to that imagined by the author previously, though I maintain that eventually class antagonisms would not have allowed such a social-democratic system of government to prevail indefinitely. Eventually labour must triumph over capital or vice versa co-existence in the political field can not last as has since been proved. However had this situation evolved it would have suited, politically, the men and women of the Irish Citizen Army perfectly because the conditions for the final victory of labour over capitalism would have existed. Who knows had the rising turned out differently it could have been the Irish Red Army, instead of the Russian variant a year or so later, we would historically speak of!.

With the death of Connolly the Irish labour movement suffered a severe blow as the British authorities began a major crackdown on the ITGWU, arresting and deporting such officials as PT Daly. 'Thomas Johnson and David Campbell, who had in no way been connected with the rising, disassociating the Labour Movement as a whole from any responsibility, demanded the immediate trial and release of the imprisoned trade unionists and the return of all books and paper seized by the military' (ibid). The ITGWU in particular had already started distancing itself from its offspring the Irish Citizen Army. The clampdown on trade unionists and their organisational affairs was well over the top, to the point of extreme, even by the standards of the British Crown. It could be argued that the Labour Movement should perhaps look back with a certain amount of shame at their attitude towards the rising particularly in view of the fact that one of their most principled leaders was executed. At a meeting in Sligo chaired by Thomas Johnson the trade union movement issued the following: 'As a Trade Union Movement we are of varied mind on matters of historical political development, and, consequently, this is not the place to enter into discussion as to the right or wrong, the wisdom or folly, of the revolt, but this we may say, that those amongst the rebels who had been associated with us in the past, who have led and inspired some of us with their love of their country and class, were led to act as they did with no selfish thought but purely with a passion for freedom and hatred of oppression' (ibid). Clearly this was a reference to the part played in the rising by James Connolly, Michael Mallin and Constance Markievicz along with the rest of the men and women of the Citizen Army.

The animosity, if this is the correct term, from the ITGWU towards the Irish Citizen Army came to a head after the rising and as Peter Berresford Ellis in quoting JD Clarkson from his book *Labour and Nationalism in Ireland*, in his own book *A History of the Irish Working Class* on page 237 from the proceedings of the 1916 Irish TUC meeting in Sligo, which brought attempts to repudiate the Citizen Army as well as the aforementioned understanding oration, Clarkson states: 'Looking at these 1916 Congress proceedings we are compelled to the conclusion that Connolly's own view of the role of the Citizen Army as the workers fighting force, received no endorsement from the Irish Trade Union Congress. Partly this was due, no doubt, to the feeling that the time was not opportune for any defiant declaration. But it must also be remembered that, even in Connolly's time, there was strong opposition to the Citizen Army using the hall (Liberty Hall) and to the association of the army with union activities'. This was the same ITUC which gave its approval to the formation of the Irish Citizen Army back in November 1913, probably because they never expected it, the army, to actually do anything more than serve as a pass time for striking or locked out workers. However Frank Robbins who was a volunteer of the Irish Citizen Army and a member of the ITGWU disputes the depth of this cleavage. In his book *Under the Starry Plough* he describes as "fiction" this hostility from the ITGWU towards the Citizen Army which originated from a dispute over whether the army should be allowed to hoist the green flag over Liberty Hall on Palm Sunday. Apparently 'a member of the branch committee named Farrell moved a resolution that Connolly be instructed not to hoist the flag as this action would be regarded by the British authorities as an open declaration of war and would possibly result in the seizure of Liberty Hall by Dublin Castle. There was a discussion on this resolution in Connolly's presence during a meeting of the No 1 Branch Committee. Eventually Connolly asked the Chairman, Thomas Foran, for permission for himself and Farrell to retire for a few moments to discuss the mater in private' (Robbins: P.58). After this private discussion between the pair Farrell asked permission to withdraw the resolution, which was granted, having been satisfied with Connolly's explanation and reasons for wishing to fly the flag. Permission was now granted to hoist the green flag and gold harp over Liberty Hall. Frank Robbins concludes: 'The Irish Citizen Army came into being as a result of the activities of the Irish Transport and General Workers Union. It could not have been created and could not have continued to exist but for the help and co-operation of the Union' (Robbins: p.59). So here we have two conflicting views on the subject but we should remember that Frank Robbins was a member of the union and volunteer of the army therefore his account should be considered first hand.

In just three short years, it is claimed by some and contradicted by others, disaffection towards the Citizen Army had grown in both the ITGWU, the parent of the army, and the ITUC. One of the problems the ITGWU may have faced in ostracizing the army during the time of James Connolly could have been the fact that he, Connolly, was the secretary of the union and Commandant of the army. Connolly could see, as a revolutionary socialist, no contradiction in wearing both hats at the same time as they complimented each other. With Connolly now dead things were changing and William O'Brien was now acting secretary of the Irish Transport and General Workers Union and, even though he was a follower of Connolly's teachings, his remit now stopped with trade union business having no say in the affairs of the Irish Citizen Army or its actions. This made it easier for the non Marxists and reformers in the union to try and distance the ITGWU from the Citizen Army without having to bother with the dual hat scenario of previous times. This was the first time since the formation of the Irish Citizen Army that the secretary of the ITGWU was not the same person as the one in charge of the Citizen Army thus giving the disciples of reform over revolution the upper hand.

To those who were, and are, critical of Connolly for leading the Irish Citizen Army into what the revisionists often term a "nationalist revolution" it is only necessary to quote VI Lenin on the subject: 'whoever expects a pure social revolution will never live to see it. Such a person pays lip service to the revolution without understanding what revolution really is' (Berresford Ellis: P234). Lenin continues: 'The struggle of the oppressed nations of Europe, a struggle capable of going to the length of insurrection and street fighting, of breaking down the iron discipline in the army and martial law, will sharpen the revolutionary crisis in Europe more than a much more developed rebellion in a remote colony. A blow delivered against the British imperialist bourgeois rule by a rebellion in Ireland is of a hundred times greater political significance than a blow of equal weight in Asia or Africa' (ibid). This oration by Lenin at the time was obviously a direct criticism of those who faulted Connolly for taking part in the rising, a criticism perhaps as well founded today as it was in the early part of the 20th century.

With the Easter Rising over the former revolutionary trend within the labour and trade union movement ended with it. The revolutionary ideas espoused by Larkin and Connolly ebbed away and gave to the reformist ideas which exist to this present day. The trade union and labour movement in Ireland, as with all other liberal democracies became an opposition within the parameters of capitalism and by now had ceased to be a mechanism for the overthrow of it. Capitalism tolerates trade unionism and labour opposition providing that their ideas do not threaten the existence of liberal democracy and the capitalist mode of production. This, of course, gives the impression of a truly democratic system with free speech and all that goes with it. However on closer examination nothing could be further from the truth. Free speech and freedom of expression are only allowed providing enough people do not take too much notice of the orators, particularly if those doing the preaching are advocates of socialism and workers control of the means of production in a truly democratic fashion. These were the ideas of Larkin, Connolly and the Citizen Army. William O'Brien, who succeeded Connolly as Secretary of the Irish Transport and General Workers Union may have been a disciple of the teachings of James Connolly but as a revolutionary leader he was not in the same league. With the death of Connolly the ITGWU preached reform as opposed to revolution or, to quote a 19th century British craft trade union, the Amalgamated Society of Engineers, "defence not defiance". This new policy of the labour and trade union movement would of course explain the distance which now existed between themselves and the Irish

Citizen Army which still held with the reality that socialism could not be achieved through reforms within the capitalist system. In other words chalk and cheese don't mix, they are inedible. In defence of jobs and living conditions if a trade union mobilises its members in defence of these and the system perceives it as a threat then the full weight of the state will be brought to bear on that particular union. Comparatively recent evidence of this can be seen with the treatment of the British Coal Miners, being battered to the ground and communities under police curfew, in their strike of 1984/85, perhaps if they had an equivalent of the Citizen Army at their disposal the outcome may have been somewhat different, who knows ?

14

THE WAR OF INDEPENDENCE AND THE IRISH CITIZEN ARMY

The war of independence had curious beginnings and its first shots were not sanctioned by the Dail. The incident which sparked the war occurred at Soloheadbeag in Co. Tipperary with the shooting of an RIC man by two volunteers, Dan Breen and Sean Treacy, who would both become legends in their own lifetimes, in 1918. This war was to differ greatly in character from the events of Easter Week, though the aims and objectives remained the same. Unlike the 1916 rising the volunteers who took part in the War of Independence, sometimes referred to as the "Anglo Irish War" conducted an urban guerrilla campaign against the crown forces amongst whose number included the infamous Black and Tans. The struggle of 1916 was, to a certain extent, a conventional war between two armed forces engaging each other on the streets of Dublin. There were other areas of conflict such as Athenry with Irish troops under the command of Liam Mellows and in Cork where activity occurred, led by the Kent family, after the surrender of Dublin. One explanation for the belated engagements in Cork was perhaps the capture of the arms ship *Aud* off the Kerry coast carrying German weapons for use in the rising which also resulted in the arrest of Sir Roger Casement, but generally the theatre of war was in Dublin.

The War of Independence was to be conducted in a different way, a winnable way for the want of a better expression, using guerrilla tactics against the conventional forces of the crown. The tactics were often referred to as "hit and run" meaning striking a blow at the enemy and disappearing. These same methods of warfare had been studied by James Connolly prior to the Easter Rising which meant that members of the Irish Citizen Army had much to offer in this conflict. The involvement of the Citizen Army was not as great as it perhaps should have been, read below for reasons, but individuals were involved and brought with them an area of expertise which otherwise may have been denied. However this ability generally only applied to those Citizen Army personnel who had been around under the stewardship of James Connolly. Many new members were not of the same calibre as the veterans of the lockout and the Easter rising.

After the rising and the execution of Connolly and Mallin the qualities possessed by some of the new volunteers entering the ranks of the Irish Citizen Army was not, in the opinion held by some of the veterans, of the same calibre as those who formed the army in 1913 and took part in the rising of 1916. Some veterans of the 1913 lockout and Easter Rising, such as Frank Robbins recognised some of the new members as people who had returned to work in 1913 on the employers terms. Other older members thought they recognised some of the new blood as those who had taken the jobs of men and women who were locked out. For these reasons some of the seasoned personnel were, at best, sceptical and at worst totally mistrusting of some of the new arrivals. It should be understood that such apprehensions occur in nearly all organisations when new people come in but what added to the tensions in the Citizen Army was that it was thought some of the new members were partly to blame for the conditions suffered by the locked out workers of 1913. How much truth and to what extent there is in this is difficult to ascertain but if only a fraction is factual then a certain amount of animosity and contempt was to be expected and certainly understood. The old maxim "once a scab always a scab" as prevalent in the ranks of organised labour today as at any other time.

With the rising over and Connolly executed James O'Neill assumed command of the Citizen Army. He was a carpenter by trade and had taken part in the events of Easter week. O'Neill however bore little if any of the political ideologies and qualities possessed by Connolly and Mallin and it was thought by some that he lacked the intelligence of both men to be even mentioned in the same sentence, it must be remembered that this was an opinion held by some and not all though nobody would have put him on the same pedestal as Connolly. He seemed to lack the basic understanding of Marxism let alone the principle of syndicalism as a means of overthrowing capitalism and the achievement of socialism. Some members of the Citizen Army blamed O'Neill for the lack of participation by the army, as an independent force, in the War Of Independence 1919-1921 and his constant prophesy that the Citizen Army should bide their time and wait for "the great day". As events unfolded there was another, more sinister reason, for O'Neill's reluctance to commit the Citizen Army to the war, a reason which was to cost him his Commandants position, reputation such as it was and any self respect. This decision not to commit the Citizen Army as a body to the war did not prevent individuals and groups of Citizen Army personnel from committing themselves to the cause. Constance Markievicz, Irish Citizen Army, was a member of the first Dail and in that assembly was appointed Minister for Labour. She still maintained her Citizen Army identity despite fighting under the broader republican umbrella commanded in Dublin by Oscar Traynor. Just as earlier members of the Irish Citizen Army were involved with sabotage activities before the Easter Rising now they were involved with under cover procurement of weaponry and intelligence gathering. The following is an extract from Patrick Kennedy, member of the Irish Citizen Army 1917, and D Company 2nd Battalion Dublin Brigade 1918: "My first association with the National Movement was in 1917 when I joined the Irish Citizen Army. About a year later I transferred to D Company, 2nd Battalion Dublin Brigade (IRA) . The late Tom Ennis was Battalion Commandant at that time, Dick McKee was Brigadier, Oscar Traynor was Vice Brigadier and Paddy Moran was my company Captain. Up until 1919 there was very little activity apart from drilling and attending lectures at night.

GHQ Intelligence

About the middle of 1920 my company O.C., Paddy Moran, sent for me and informed me that I had been selected as a suitable man for G.H.Q. Intelligence work. He took me to Oriel Hall in Oriel street and there introduced me to Tom Cullen, Liam Tobin and Frank Thornton. They informed me that I had been selected for intelligence work. They pointed out how dangerous and secret this work was, and that if I was prepared to undertake it I would have to leave my employment as it was full time work. I told them that I understood the conditions and that I was quite willing to take on any duties allotted to me.

I took up duty almost immediately and reported to Crow Street, and there Frank Thornton gave me my instructions. I was to contact a number of agents who were working under the British Crown, and thereafter I was to keep in contact with them and convey any information they would give me to the Intelligence Department. Some of the principle agents I was introduced to were Dave Neligan, Reynolds the Auxiliary, and Ned Broy. Others of lesser importance were a waiter in the Gresham Hotel, a porter in the Shelbourne Hotel and a civilian working in the telephone exchange in Parkgate Street, headquarters of the Dublin command"(Perhaps the latter part of this statement highlights, to a certain extent the difference of expression between the Citizen Army as a body where all personnel were of equal importance, and the terminology caught on by working in the Dublin Brigade, "lesser importance". This is an observation by the author and not necessarily a statement of fact). This kind of work was of vital importance in the prosecution of the war because the republican forces were greatly outnumbered and outgunned so gaining an advantage through intelligence work was essential.

Patrick Kennedy's statement continues "I can not recall the type of information that Dave Neligan or Ned Broy passed out but I do remember the nature of information that we received from Reynolds. Reynolds reported the conversation of the Auxiliaries describing how they had carried out shootings, who carried them out and who the ringleaders were. He gave us full details of to the perpetrators of the murder of Ned Clancy, Dick McKee and Clune. He told us that these three men were kicked and beaten first in order to extract information from them. The authorities did not succeed in getting anything from the three men, and as a result they were shot in the Castle". (Courtesy National Archives W/S 499).

Information such as that briefly outlined above was extremely helpful in tracking down these legalised murderers and obviously organising retaliatory action. This is just one example of the numerous roles played by Citizen Army personnel during the War of Independence even though, unlike 1916, they were not organised as the Irish Citizen Army the autonomous identity of Citizen Army personnel was maintained. The above incident was in no way an isolated occurrence as Citizen Army personnel were involved in many more intelligence actions during the War of Independence. Christopher Crothers was one such volunteer of the Citizen Army attached to such work. "About the beginning of March 1920 a friend of my grandmother, Miss Kate Murphy, was employed in a house numbered 15 Upper Fitzwilliam Street. Miss Murphy approached me one evening when she was visiting the house and told me that twelve men had taken up residence in the house where she was employed. She thought that they were ex British officers because of the fact that one man to whom the others appeared to look up to was a man who had lost an arm in the Great War. He was known as Captain Bennett. I asked her if she was sure they were ex officers and she said she could not be certain. She said they were all acting as commercial traveller's. What they were travelling for she did not know, with the exception of Bennett, she knew, was travelling for Irish Horn Beads. I asked her why she came to me with this story and she told me that while these men were supposed to be commercial travellers they never went out in the day time; that the earliest they left the house was 5 O'Clock in the evening and they were not back when she returned".

There was obviously something suspicious about these men particularly with the war at its height, British agents could have been and, indeed were, everywhere. Crothers decided to report this matter to his commanding officer, Captain Robert De Coeur of the Irish Citizen Army. Crothers continues "I understand that Captain De Coeur gave my report to the O/C, intelligence Dublin Brigade. As a result of this Captain De Coeur instructed me to keep a very close watch on the house, number 15 Upper Fitzwilliam Street, and if possible get into it when these men were absent. After this I had several conversations with Miss Murphy who gave me reports concerning the times these men left the house and when they returned. They always left between 5 and 7pm. They were never seen leaving together: they generally left in ones and twos and on some occasions they did not leave the house until very late at night. All these matters I reported to Captain De Coeur. Sometime between the months of May and June one morning the Citizens of Dublin awoke to the sight of, posted on most of the tram and lamp standards in the city a small bill-headed purporting to have been issued by the Catholic Bishops with reference to association with the IRA, Sinn Fein and kindred organisations. The bill-head was approximately 6" by 4". These bill-heads were not issued by the Catholic Bishops at all but were the work of the authorities. An attempt by the British authorities to play on peoples devotion to the Roman Catholic faith to divorce the population from the republican cause. Christopher Crothers continues: "That evening Miss Murphy came to me with three or four of the posters and informed me that the men staying at the house had hundreds of these posters and were out all night posting them up throughout the city". As instructed by Captain De Coeur Crothers went to the house, accompanied by Miss Murphy, when the strangers were out and, on gaining entry, found hundreds of the offending posters on top of a wardrobe in the front drawing room. It would be imagined that this was very complacent of the men to leave such evidence in such a conspicuous place maybe, for some reason, they underestimated the high level of support which existed among the Irish population for the republican cause. Cristopher Crothers took a number of these posters to Captain De Coeur who immediately took him and the posters to the O/C intelligence Dublin Brigade. As a result of this meeting Crothers was instructed to watch the house and to report more regularly what was happening there. The statement continues: "A few weeks later I was instructed to keep away from the house but at the same time I was to keep in close contact with Miss Murphy. About the month of August Miss Murphy told me the men were leaving the house in a few days. I asked her where did she get the information. She told me that Captain Bennett told her they were going. I then asked her how did it occur to her that he spoke to her and gave her this information and she told me that she had occasion to go into his room that morning and he started to jeer her about her friends and told her that he was leaving and that her friends would find it very hard to find him" (statement by Christopher Crothers, Irish Citizen Army, W/S 759; courtesy National Archives).

Judging by this last statement from Bennett it would appear that the Republican Intelligence Officers watching the house were themselves under surveillance. All the men left very shortly afterwards, breaking up thus making it harder to trace them. It was noted by Miss Murphy, the night before these commercial travellers were leaving, that every man was armed which was strange to say the least for men claiming to be in such an occupation. Miss Murphy knew about the men's weaponry because on the eve of their departure they had a drinking session and two of them got so drunk that they shot up the wash basin. A few months later when the republican intelligence network was at its height, under the stewardship of Michael Collins, these men's actions would almost certainly have cost them their lives. This was a relatively low key piece of intelligence work involving a volunteer of the Irish Citizen Army and his officer commanding, Captain De Coeur, and working in concert with the overall command of the Dublin Brigade.

During the War of Independence intelligence work was not the only covert operations undertook by the Irish Citizen Army, the procurement of weapons was another avenue which they were involved in. On some occasions they procured weaponry with the collusion of sympathetic British personnel. At the outbreak of World War1 Edward Hanley was serving with the 4th Battalion Dublin Fusiliers. In 1916 Hanley was on sick leave having received wounds in France. He went absent but was unfortunately captured and reduced from Sergeant to Private. Edward Hanley was to become of particular use to the Citizen Army in his role as a store man at Portebello Barracks in Dublin. He could not return to the front because of his injuries but could carry out lighter duties such as those of a store man. It was in this capacity which was to be of use to the Citizen Army for the procurement of rifles and revolvers, presumably for what Commandant James O'Neill kept referring to as the "great day for the Citizen Army", a day which was sadly intended to be a great day for O'Neill and nobody else which, as we shall see, was uncovered by the Citizen Army and cost O'Neill his position.

According to Edward Hanley's own account of the procurement of these rifles and revolvers: "James (Skiver) Keogh and later James O'Shea and Matt Burke asked me what were the chances of getting some rifles and revolvers from Portobello. I told Keogh I could take them out if I could get a suitable turnscrew to enable me to take the rifles to pieces. Keogh who worked on the railway at inchicore made me one and I was able to carry out the stripped rifles. Later I was able to pass rifles out through the railings at the sports field to Citizen Army men waiting in Mount Thomond Avenue near Harolds Cross. To do this I had to elude the sentries near the sports field. James O'Shea was one of the persons to whom the rifles were passed out in this way. Barney Craven, I remember, was the driver of the cab in which the rifles were taken away.

The authorities knew that the rifles were been taken but I was never suspected. They had come to the conclusion that the rifles were being taken out in traders vans and used to conduct periodical searches of these vans.

I was later transferred to a newly formed Labour Corps at Wellington Barracks where I was again able to pass out rifles at the back gate near Harolds Cross Bridge. A military policeman who had been transferred from Portobello with me knew what I was doing and was sympathetic. I always chose the time he was on duty at the back gate to pass out the rifles. In Wellington Barracks there were huts where men used to go for lectures on wet days. They often left their rifles outside the huts and it was an easy matter to take a few. As I was a store man I did not attract undue attention when walking around with the rifles. The men, of course, had to pay for the lost rifles and this generally seemed to satisfy the authorities, although there were periodical searches of trades vans here also. My Military Policeman friend always gave me notice of any searches that were to take place.

About 1920 when a number of troops were coming home on leave, were either selling their rifles or having them taken from them, the authorities built a hut at North wall and collected the rifles, later to be transferred to Ship Street Barracks. I even got about five or six from the Black and Tans stationed there. The Black and Tans were very often drunk so it was easy to take a rifle now and again" (extract from statement Edward Hanley 12th December 1951: courtesy National Archives). As can be seen from this statement it was easy for the Citizen Army to acquire weapons in this way. It was just a mater of knowing which personnel working for the Crown were in some way sympathetic. What is surprising and in many ways how lax in security the authorities were particularly when it came to rifles going missing.

Frank Robbins, an Irish Citizen Army volunteer, had a low opinion of James O'Neill as a Commandant, which was the same as his view of him as a person whom he suspected of a certain underhandedness later to be proved well founded. Robbins, along with other Citizen Army personnel, was furious that they were not more involved in the war as an independent armed force and particularly their non involvement in the attack carried out on the Customs House by the Volunteers (hereon referred to as the Irish Republican Army, IRA). This assault was a morale booster for the IRA in the War of Independence and as much as it boosted the spirits of the IRA it dampened those of the British Crown. Frank Robbins and his comrades believed that the Irish Citizen Army should have been given the opportunity to take part in this attack and not be held back by their own commandant. This was just one act of, at best indecisiveness, and, at worst self preservation by O'Neill which infuriated many volunteers of the Irish Citizen Army. Much frustration was setting in within the ranks of the Citizen Army and many personnel went to fight as individuals and groups under the command of the IRA while maintaining their Citizen Army autonomous identity. As the Irish Citizen Army was confined to the Dublin area, so far as membership was recruited, their personnel came under the overall command of Oscar Traynor, O/C republican forces for the Dublin area. For people like Frank Robbins the fact that the Citizen Army were not involved in the war in their own right and under their own command structure was a bitter pill to swallow. However the prevailing view was that it was better to be involved, albeit under another organisations structure, than not to be active at all and they were, after all, recognised as Citizen Army personnel. Another issue tormented some Irish Citizen Army personnel regarding this arrangement with the IRA and that was, outside the goal of removing British rule from Irish soil, there was no clear political objective as to what form the new independent republic would take. From the point of view taken by the volunteers of the Irish Citizen Army, who were revolutionary socialists, nothing short of a republic bearing the socialist title and political content would suffice. This would of course include nationalisation of all large industry under workers control and one state run bank. All financial institutions would again be under state control and all the means of production, distribution and exchange under workers control and common ownership. On the other hand many of those with whom they were fighting alongside were far from socialist in their outlook, in fact many were vehemently capitalist. Once again the echoes of Connolly's oration prior to the Easter Rising about holding on to weapons must have been bouncing off the ear drums of some Citizen Army veterans. Examples of this political diversity which existed in the republican ranks would be the politics of the veteran 1913 Trojan Constance Markievicz, who was to be appointed Minister for Labour in the first Dail and a strong disciple of James Connolly's Marxist position and those of WT Cosgrave, whom she fought alondside, and who was to become the President Of The Executive Council in the first *Saorstat* (Free State) government and was a strong supporter of the capitalist system. These are just two examples of contradicting political positions, which can never be reconciled, within the broad church of republicanism. One irony of this political diversity was that Constance Markievicz, the rampant socialist, did much election campaigning for WT Cosgrave in the 1918 General Election.

Another irony surrounding the revolutionary events in Ireland 1919-21 was the great faith which the republican government in exile, so to speak, placed in the United States of America regarding recognition of the fledgling republic. People like Harry Boland and Eamonn De Valera travelled to the USA in order to petition President Woodrow Wilson for recognition of Ireland as an independent nation state. Wilson's attitude towards Irelands claim was negative to say the least. He and Congress refused Irelands claim, or to even support such a claim, on the grounds that Great Britain was a friendly country and was allied to the USA. The United States, then as now, refused to come to Irelands aid in the form of recognising the republic and thus putting pressure on Britain to grant independence. In sharp contrast to the position adopted by the USA regarding this recognition the fledgling country of socialist intentions, Soviet Russia, gave almost instant recognition to Irelands claim and thus the fledgling republic. Perhaps this should have sent out a message to the Irish revolutionaries that they were playing the wrong game with the wrong team in relying on the pro capitalist United States for support. Maybe it would have been a better idea to swap their Stars and Stripes wishful thinking for the Red Flag reality of socialism and Soviet Russia for aid. To this day the government of the 26 independent (to a certain degree) Southern counties still think they have some kind of special relationship with the United States of America, a relationship which quite frankly (outside some family connections) does not exist except in so far as the USA says jump and Ireland says how high.

A couple of years before Eamon De Valera and Harry Boland went out to the USA to petition President Wilson Frank Robbins, Irish Citizen Army, was also in that country trying to build up support for the cause, though not at Presidential level. Towards the end of 1917 Robbins met with Liam mellows, IRA, in the United States and the conversation drifted in the direction of conscription being introduced in Ireland to provide more cannon fodder for Britain's war effort. Frank Robbins decided it was time to return to Ireland and he eventually found a ship, the *St. Paul*, where he was employed to earn his ticket in the engine room with the help of a Mr Lynch who was the secretary of the Seamens Union in new York. The *St. Paul*, with Frank Robbins installed on board, slipped its birth on the 15th February 1918 destination Liverpool.

On his arrival at Liverpool, carrying revolvers in the bottom of his bag, Frank Robbins faced a situation he could have done without and had to bluff his way passed a policeman claiming he was going to change his clothes at his sisters house before returning to New York. Fortunately the policeman swallowed the lie and waved Robbins through. 'Barry O'Hea, an Irishman and an official of the National Seamen and Firemen's Union, helped us out with digs that night and the following day we paid a visit to the shop on Scotland Road of a man named Murphy, a famous old stalwart in Irelands fight for freedom' *Under The Starry Plough; Recollections of the Irish Citizen Army*: Frank Robbins P.198). Frank Robbins left Liverpool taking the longer, at least by land, Hollyhead route and arrived back in Dublin on 1st March 1918 where he almost immediately made contact with Michael Collins at the premises for National Aid on Batchelors Walk where he informed Collins of the activities engaged by Melows and others in New York to procure arms for Ireland. On hearing this Collins was eager to maintain contact with Robbins but this was to prove difficult due to the considerable antipathy which had once again surfaced between the Citizen Army and the Volunteers. 'As a result of this situation I was to find myself, in the years following, torn between my loyalty to my comrades in the Citizen Army on the one hand and my loyalty to Liam Mellows and my other friends in the Volunteers on the other' (Robbins: P.198-199). The old mistrust which had existed between the Irish Citizen Army and the Irish Volunteers, latterly IRA, had never quite evaporated despite bearing arms side by side for the duration of Easter Week.

One of Frank Robbins first tasks on his return to Ireland was to contact his old colleagues in the Irish Citizen Army. He recalls, 'I had an early opportunity of discussing the affairs of the Army with Michael Donnelly, Michael Kelly, James O'Shea and others of my former comrades. Somewhat to my discomforiture (sic) I found that the situation was anything but akin to that of the pre-1916 period. There was a new atmosphere, a new outlook, entirely different from that which had been moulded by Connolly and Mallin. Many of those who had been recruited into the Army during my absence seemed to lack the spirit, the understanding and the discipline which were so characteristic in the earlier period' (Robbins: P. 201). The reader will recall earlier that many veterans in the Irish Citizen Army were less than pleased with the new leadership and some of the new recruits. Relations between the ITGWU and the Irish Citizen Army had been strained to say the least after the rising, with the Citizen Army being asked to leave Liberty Hall, the place of its birth. However on Robbins return to Dublin any flimsy co-operation between the two had disappeared completely. The situation could be described, certainly to the casual observer at the time, as open hostility from the former towards the latter.

Many of the women who taken part in the 1916 rising had by now left the Citizen Army. Much of the blame for this departure lie in the fact that some of the new members recruited into the women's section had a very dubious background as far as trade union loyalties were concerned. The fact that some of these recruits had worked during the 1913 lockout was deeply resented by women who had lost their jobs fighting to uphold trade unionism. A resentment which any trade unionist today should well understand and sympathise with.

The new commandant of the Irish Citizen Army, as the reader will recall, was a carpenter by trade named James O'Neill. Frank Robbins continues 'I regarded him as being chiefly responsible for the post - insurrection situation and left him in no doubt as to my view point. His failure was entirely due to his lack or desire to pursue the Connolly philosophy. When questions of policy arose O'Neill's attitude was to procrastinate rather than take the line which would have been laid down by Connolly and Mallin, were they there to lead. The kernel of the problem was that without such a man to guide the organisation the majority of the newer members, strange as it may seem, did not hold or advocate the social and political views that had motivated those who fought in 1916 and which were responsible for the courage and tenacity the men and women displayed in many actions during that historic week of struggle' (Robbins: P.202).

At this time, and given the changing circumstances, there were those on the Army Council of the Irish Citizen Army, and Frank

Robbins was one, who advocated greater co-operation between themselves and the IRA. Equally there was much opposition to this stance, the most common argument against being that the Volunteers, 'as a result of IRB activities, had been, and still were, endeavouring to bring about the absorption of the Citizen Army into the larger organisation and so bring it under IRB control' (Robbins: P. 203). It could be argued that there was a certain amount of truth in this assertion. If the reader will recall Connolly had stated, at least publicly, that there "were no longer an Irish Citizen Army or Irish Volunteers but one Army of the Irish Republic". However it will also be remembered that privately Connolly also stated "in the event of victory hold on to your rifles, as those with whom we are fighting may stop before our goal is reached. We are out for economic as well as political liberty". In his book, *The Life and Times of James Connolly*, C. Desmond Greaves, as a footnote, suggests "those with whom we are fighting" could at the time be a reference to MacNeill, etc. 'It would be mistaken to read here an attitude to Pearse and Clarke, with whom Connolly was in collusion' (Greaves, foot note; P 403). This assesment by Greaves of Connolly's statement I fundamentally disagree with on the basis that Connolly made this oration on the evening of Palm Sunday by which time he had managed to ideologically separate the Pearse and MacDonagh, the progressive faction with political limitations, away from MacNeill. MacNeill was, at the time, unaware of the rising and was not involved in any way with the plans to execute the event drawn up by the IRB members. Only at a time closer to the rising did he, through informants information, become alerted to what was about to occur. If he had been aware it follows he would have opposed it, as he felt the time was not ripe, so much so that when he did find out he issued a statement to cancel all manoeuvres by the Volunteers for Sunday 23rd April. If MacNeill was unaware of the plans right up until the last minuet, when he made it clear he was having nothing to do with it, how could he have been one of "those with whom we are fighting"?. Connolly was indeed referring to Pearse, McDonagh etc with this statement. If MacNeill had his way there would have been no Easter Rising. So back to the debate within the Citizen Army regarding greater co-operation with the Volunteers in 1918, which had strong echoes of the past. The former public statement made by Connolly, back in 1916, would point towards greater co-operation if not integration, and the latter private oration would strongly point in the direction of Citizen Army autonomy. Unfortunately Connolly was no longer around to clarify his exact position but as can be gleaned it was not a new scenario and is one which still provides contrasting interpretations for debate.

James O'Neill was opposed to any form of greater co-operation on the grounds, so he claimed, that such a move would almost certainly lead to absorption. However as we shall see there was a more sinister motive for O'Neills opposition. O'Neill's opposition to the stance taken by the co-operationists was to lead to a considerable amount of inaction during the War of Independence by the Irish Citizen Army as a body. As Frank Robbins puts it 'why was the Citizen Army not involved in the attack of the 12th April, 1921, on the London North Western Railway Hotel near Spencer Dock on the North Wall?. This building was a strong link in the lines of communication of the Auxiliaries' (Robbins: P.206). Another missed opportunity of offensive action in the war was the attack and subsequent burning of the Custom House, close to Liberty Hall also in 1921. Some unemployed members of the Citizen Army were sat on some steps within a stones throw of the Custom House unaware of the attack going on inside which once again yielded favourable results. These are merely two missed opportunities experienced by the more than eager volunteers of the Irish Citizen Army due to O'Neill's stewardship. Frank Robbins was correct to question why the Citizen Army had not been involved in the attack which had satisfactory results for republican forces. The post was badly damaged by rifle fire and bombs and therefore from the point of view of the British whose prestige had been badly dented it was a set back. O'Neill's leadership totally lacked the political principles and vision possessed by

Connolly and Mallin. This leadership deficiency of O'Neill's leading to inaction was to prove costly to the Citizen Army, for it meant that a unique opportunity was forfeited by them, the military arm of labour, to have any influence in the political reshaping of future Ireland.

It was badly calculated decisions such as the ones outlined above which partially led to O'Neills demise as Commandant of the Irish Citizen Army. There were other, more serious, issues connected to his eventual dismissal and according to Frank Robbins: 'In the oft professed view of Commandant O'Neill the Citizen Army must be kept in tact for the big day that was surely coming. Little we knew then of O'Neill's efforts at self aggrandizement, or we would have been less content to accept this slogan. It is no part of my intention to go into the whole sad story that eventually led to O'Neill's dismissal from his command and his conviction before the courts. One of these concerned the acquisition of twelve rifles by the South Tipperary Brigade of the IRA. As we understood the situation the rifles were to be the gift of the Citizen Army to Tipperary's gallant fighters, the Citizen Army Council had so decided, and it was almost by accident that a very different state of things was revealed. One day I had met Sean Russell who I had been with in Knutsford and Frongoch and was now on the headquarters staff of the IRA. We discussed O'Neill and some matters which had come to our attention. I mentioned how much we were inhibited in our approach to some of our Commandants dealings by the fact that he was on the headquarters staff of the IRA and then went on to speak of the Citizen Army's gift of the rifles to Tipperary. To my complete surprise Russell vehemently denied that O'Neill had any position on the GHQ staff and, as for the rifles, the Tipperary Brigade had bought them from O'Neill. This information came as a great shock to me and I determined to have the affair probed as deeply as I could' (Robbins: P.215). Through Russell Robbins met Oscar Traynor, O/C Dublin Brigade, and it was agreed that Traynor would obtain a written statement from Sean McMahon, Quartermaster General, confirming the sale of the rifles to the Tipperary Brigade. After some time Russell informed Robbins that Traynor had the confirming document and he was welcome to access it. The statement was evidence that the rifles had indeed been sold by O'Neill, for personal gain, to the Tipperary Brigade. This was the more sinister incident often referred to throughout which was to terminate the career of James O'Neill as Commandant of the Irish Citizen Army. 'The Army Council decided not only to remove O'Neill from the position of commandant but to set up a court-martial to try him on a number of charges. Doctor Kathleen Lynn was appointed Chairman of the court. While the court-martial was proceeding the Truce took place and the civilian authorities under existing law proceeded against O'Neill, who was arrested on a number of charges, convicted and sent to prison' (Robbins: P. 216). Nobody who supports the system which we have come to know as capitalism, based on profit and pure self interest has any right to criticise O'Neill because he was only acting as the employing class act, then as now, every day. However the members of the Irish Citizen Army do not number amongst this pro capitalist clique and had every right to act, if they felt fit, as judge, jury and executioner. Frank Robbins reward for the revelations he had uncovered leading to the dismissal of O'Neill was promotion to the rank of Lieutenant in the Irish Citizen Army.

As we come to the end of this chapter on the War of Independence the reader should be reminded that even though, through the instructions of O'Neill, the Irish Citizen Army, as a single united organisation, took no part in the war individuals and groups from the organisation certainly did. Even though these people, based in Dublin due to the parochial provincial membership of their organisation, were under the central command of the IRA they did maintain their autonomous identity throughout. The leadership of the Irish Citizen Army were not involved in the peace talks of 1921, even though they had representation at cabinet level of the first Dail in the form of Constance Markievicz, Minister for Labour, and non were signatories to the treaty signed on 6th December 1921 between an Irish delegation headed, by Michael Collins and Arthur Griffith, and a British delegation headed by David Lloyd George (Prime Minister) and Winston Churchill. This treaty was to divide the republican forces into pro and anti treaty camps and lead to Civil war in Ireland, 1922-23.

15

THE IRISH CITIZEN ARMY
AND THE CIVIL WAR

The civil war which engulfed Ireland, following the signing of the treaty, in 1922-23 was not a good thing irrespective of a any particular view point. The only people who benefited were the Loyalists in the North and of course the British. In fact the civil war could almost have been engineered by David Lloyd George, the Welsh Wizard, himself with Michael Collins and Eamonn De Valera and their respective followers fighting it out with each other. Watching this show were the British Government pretending to support the new Irish Free State, *Saorstat Eireann*, all the time knowing that they, the British could not lose. If the Republican forces won the British would have reoccupied and if *Saorstat Eireann* had won, which turned out to be the case, well the country would be organised as a mirror image of the Westminster model and just in case this turned out not to be the case, well, reinvasion and occupation was always the puppet masters option.

The treaty signed on 6th December, 1921, between the British and Irish delegations giving 26 of Ireland's 32 counties dominion status along with the British insistence of Ireland retaining the oath to the Crown, which read: 'I....do solemnly swear true faith and allegiance to the constitution of the Irish Free State as by law established and that I will be faithful to HM King George V, his heirs and successors by law, in virtue of the common citizenship of Ireland with Great Britain and her adherence to the membership of the group of nations forming the British Commonwealth of Nations' (*The Civil War 1922-23*: Eoin Neeson: P.313). This may be an opportunity to explain the difficulties faced by the Irish delegation in London at the time. Firstly Michael Collins, the often perceived villain of the day, had a 10,000 sovereigns price tag on his head and would anybody believe that had he not signed the treaty he would have seen Ireland again? This man the British had no idea what he looked like, until now, and now they'd got him after years hunting the fugitive. Secondly Arthur Griffith was never in fact a republican, he favoured a dual monarchist approach similar to Austria/Hungary. The main crime was not the actual signing the treaty but, as far as the Irish working class were concerned, running the country as a mirror image of those who had just left, the British. The same exploitation, degradation and ignorance which had prevailed in the days of occupation carried on unabated, except this time the governing class were Irish. However the two main problems which caused the civil war were not these but partition and the oath, not necessarily combined. Under the treaty six of the province of Ulsters nine counties were to be partitioned from the rest of the country, this was one bone of republican discontent including the Irish Citizen Army who did combine this with the detested oath, others could reluctantly live with the oath but not partition. This arrangement, partition, was to be reviewed by a commission 'consisting of three persons, one to be appointed by the Government of the Irish State, another to be appointed by the Government of Northern Ireland and one who shall be Chairman to be appointed by the British Government' (*The Civil War 1922-23*: Eoin Neeson: P.315). This arrangement was, by de-facto, permanent as the Northern Government had (have) the right of veto and remains in place to this day. It is not the intention here to go into every single detail of the Treaty but merely to point out that it was a partial victory for the Irish bourgeoisie and a disaster for the Irish Labour Movement which the Citizen Army were only too aware of.

James Connolly, not a great supporter of Home Rule per se because it did not give full independence, wrote as far back as 21st March 1914, after partition was first suggested, in *Forward*: "Here in Ireland the proposal of the Government to consent to the partition of Ireland - the exclusion of certain counties in Ulster - is causing a new line of cleavage. Not one of the supporters of Home Rule accepts this proposal with anything like equanimity, but rather we are already hearing in North-East Ulster rumours of a determination to resist it by all means. It is felt that the proposal to leave the Home Rule minority at the mercy of an ignorant majority with the evil record of the Orange party is a proposal that should never have been made, and that the establishment of such a scheme should be resisted with armed force if necessary.

Personally I entirely agree with those who think so; Belfast is bad enough as it is; what it would be under such rule the wildest imagination can not conceive. Filled with the belief that they were defeating the Imperial Government and the Nationalists combined, the Orangemen would have scant regards for the rights of the minority left at their mercy.

Such a scheme would destroy the labour movement by disrupting it. It would perpetuate in a form aggravated in evil the discords now prevalent, and help the Home Rule and Orange capitalists and clerics to keep their rallying cries before the public as the political watchword of the day. In short it would make division more intense and confusion of ideas and parties more confounded". The reasons outlined by Connolly along with the oath were the main reasons for Irish Citizen Army opposition to the treaty. There were many in the IRA, though by no means all, whose main opposition was the swearing of allegiance to the British Crown with much less emphasis than the Citizen Army on the labour question.

There are those historians such as Peter Berresford Ellis who claim, with some justification, that the Irish Civil War signalled the demise of the Citizen Army. Winston Churchill was applying pressure on *Saorstat Eireann* to take action against that section of the IRA which supported the republic. This section included the men and women who made up the ranks of the Irish Citizen Army. Churchill stated: 'The presence in Dublin of a band of men styling themselves the Headquarters of the Republic Executive is a gross breach and defiance of the treaty. The time has come when it is not unfair, premature or impatient for us to make this strengthened Irish Government and new Irish Parliament a request in express terms that this sort of thing must come to an end. If it does not come to an end, if through weakness, want of courage, or some less creditable reason it is not brought to an end, and a speedy end, then it is my duty to say, on behalf of His Majesty's Government, that we shall regard the Treaty as having been formally violated, that we shall take no steps to carry out or legalise its further stages, and that we shall resume full liberty of action in any direction that may seem proper, to any extent that may be necessary to safeguard the interests and the rights that are entrusted to our care' (Berresford Ellis: P. 261).

By this Churchill meant, in simple language, if you don't take action against these republicans then we will. Therefore under this threat, of what amounted to the reoccupation of Ireland, at 7 minuets past 4am on July 22nd 1922 the forces of *Saorstat Eireann* began the bombardment of the Four Courts in Dublin where the republican forces, including some volunteers of the Irish Citizen Army were entrenched, using artillery loaned to them by the benevolent Churchill. The Irish Citizen Army as a force were almost exclusively recruited from the ranks of the Dublin working class and 'when the Four Courts fell the Citizen Army ceased to function as it was confined to Dublin now in *Saorstat* hands' (Berresford Ellis: P.261). It should be recorded that there had been attempts to extend the membership of the Citizen Army to cover the whole country however, unfortunately, these well intentioned plans came to nothing and had they done so the bombardment of the Four Courts and seizure of vital documents would not have been such a severe blow. There may be some truth in the conclusion drawn by Peter Berresford Ellis but for descriptive reasons it would not, in my opinion, be an appropriate end as there were appearances from the Citizen Army long after the Civil War ended.

Similar to the War of Independence the participation of the Irish Citizen Army on the anti treaty side in the Civil War was very much on an individual or group basis, though it must be expressed that there were members who took no part at all in the Civil War. In other words individual members from the ranks of the Citizen Army may have taken a conscious decision to be active or not in these hostilities. Likewise groups of conferring volunteers did likewise, again both maintaining their Citizen Army identity. As previously they fell under the overall command structure of the IRA (or irregulars as *Saorstat Eireann* referred to them) now led nationally by Liam Lynch. Citizen Army members were active as commando units attached to the IRA in the Wicklow Mountains and adjoining terrain. It would be accurate to say that with the fall of the Four Courts coupled with the seizure of documents by *Saorstat* forces a severe blow was suffered by the Irish Citizen Army. The capturing of the documents led 'to the round up in Dublin of all Citizen Army men who were active and their eventual imprisonment in No.2 Internment Camp at the Curragh' (Berresford Ellis: P.261). The bombing and capturing of the Four Courts along with the seizure of important documents by the forces of *Saorstat Eireann* was a major set back for the Citizen Army and cut short the involvement for most volunteers in the Civil War. This did not mean the same as the formal end of the Citizen Army because when the order to dump arms came from Frank Aiken, who assumed command of the republican forces after the fatal shooting of Liam Lynch, they who had not been rounded up, like everybody else just went home. The Irish Citizen Army would be seen parading again on the streets of Dublin.

16

THE IRISH CITIZEN ARMY
AFTER THE CIVIL WAR

With the Civil War at an end and, as far as the republicans were concerned a less than satisfactory end at that, the Citizen Army, like their IRA counterparts simply dumped arms and went home. There was no formal surrender to the enemy or handing over, or "decommissioning", of weaponry the republican forces simply dumped arms when Frank Aiken, who had assumed command after the death of Liam Lynch, ordered them to do so and went home. Both the IRA and the Irish Citizen Army were now about to enter the twilight years though over future decades the IRA would again wage war against the British occupiers of the North on many occasions. However for the volunteers of the Citizen Army who took part in the Civil War those were to be the last shots, in most cases, fired in anger. The next time the Citizen Army were to be seen as an organisation on the streets of Dublin was to be in 1927. The occasion for their mobilisation was the funeral of Constance Markievicz, who died on July 15th . 'Thousands lined the streets; the official organisations marched: *Sinn Fein, Fianna Eireann, Inghinidhe na Eireann, Cumann na mBan, Fianna Fail*, ITGWU, Citizen Army' (*The Rebel Countess* Anne Marreco: P.300). Her Citizen Army uniform was lowered into her grave at Glasnevin cemetery where the forces of *Saorstat Eireann* were present to prevent the Citizen Army firing a volley of shots over her grave.

Also in 1927, five days before the death of Constance Markievicz the Minister for Justice, in the Cumann na nGaedhael, *Saorstat,* government who were now the Executive of the Irish Free State, Kevin O'Higgins had been shot dead by the IRA on his way to Mass. The two were the most bitter enemies and had Constance lived she would have shed no tears over the death of O'Higgins.

The two deaths highlighted the divisions which still were prevalent four years after the Civil War ended, and some would argue that these divisions are, in many cases, still alive today. Half the country was mourning the death of Kevin O'Higgins while the other half mourned the passing of Constance.

From its inception in November 1913 the Irish Citizen Army had grown and matured from being a workers defence force under their first Commandant, Jim Larkin, against the excess violence meted out by the DMP and RIC to a well disciplined revolutionary socialist army of organised labour. J. Dunsmore Clarkson described it as "the first Red Army in modern Europe". After Jim Larkin's departure to the United States of America in 1914 James Connolly took over the reins of General Secretary of the ITGWU and Commandant General of the Irish Citizen Army. As in the case of Larkin, who also held both positions, it was useful for Connolly to wear both hats because he was one of the few men capable of reconciling any differences or conflict of interests between the union and the armed wing of organised labour. Under Connolly's stewardship the Citizen Army was guided and moulded into a revolutionary force capable of waging war, if necessary single handed, against the British forces of imperialism and occupation. Connolly with his second in command, Michael Mallin, and the more than able Constance Markievicz along with the equally dedicated rank and file volunteers welded together a solidarity and bond of trust within the ranks of the Citizen Army second to none. When the Easter Rising began, 24th April 1916, it was the volunteers of the Irish Citizen Army who were the first into action at the City Hall under the command of Captain Sean Connolly (no relation to James). From the early days of being the defenders of the proletariat the Citizen Army had graduated into the realms of manufacturing their own arms and improvising other models of armoury to suit their purpose and needs at Liberty Hall. It had its own medical department headed by Dr Kathleen Lynn who gave lectures on first aid and was first called into service to tend the wounds of Captain Sean Connolly at the City Hall.

Like with all armies, the Citizen Army being no exception, mistakes were made. For example the failure to capture the Shelbourne Hotel at St. Stephens Green in 1916 was to prove a military blunder, as was the overestimation of the defence strength at Dublin Castle resulting in a lost opportunity to capture this strategically and psychologically important position. These things happen and unfortunately for the Irish Citizen Army, unlike their conventional counterparts on the British side, they only got the one opportunity.

After the Easter Rising and the executions of Connolly and Mallin the Citizen Army were for a time leaderless. Eventually James O'Neill was appointed Commandant and, as we have seen, lacked the political ideology of revolutionary Marxism and dedication to the cause of achieving the political and military aims and objectives possessed by Connolly, Mallin and Markievicz. Many of the new recruits who came in after the rising were not, in the opinion of some veterans, of the same calibre as those who were involved in the 1913 lockout and the Easter Rising. Maybe some of the criticisms aimed at many of the new recruits were a little harsh on the part of the more seasoned comrades within the organisation because, to be fair, they performed a hard act to follow. It should be remembered that these veterans had been through, in little more than two and a half years, the long and bitter dispute of 1913 and the Easter Rising of 1916 and to expect anybody to step into these shoes was raising the bar of expectations very high indeed. However some of the resentment and mistrust towards elements of the newcomers was justified especially towards those suspected of scabbing, or strike breaking, during the class struggle of 1913. Then, as now, "once a scab always a scab", ask any former Steelworker or Coal Miner in the former industrial North of England.

During the Anglo Irish War, 1919-21, some of the men and women volunteers bravely went over the head of their Commandant, James O'Neill, and took an active part in the war. This was despite O'Neill refusing any form of greater co-operation with the IRA and therefore holding back from participation by the Citizen Army, as an army, in the war. Irish Citizen Army personnel were involved in operations to procure weaponry along with intelligence work and commando actions and many other covert and overt operations. The decisions taken by Citizen Army combatants to ignore O'Neill's instructions and co-operate with the IRA were bold and, as events were to prove, correct.

During the tragic Civil War which engulfed Ireland between 1922-23, and in the imagination still exists in the minds of some, many members of the Irish Citizen Army attached themselves to the Anti-treaty wing of the now split IRA and fought bravely against the forces of *Saorstat Eireann*. Others, such as Frank Robbins, took no part in these hostilities and took a conscious decision not to do so. It was during the Civil War that the idea to extend the membership of the Citizen Army to cover the whole country was talked about. At a meeting to discuss this proposal of extending the membership of the Citizen Army across the country, one reason being, to counter the growth of militarism and to ensure that workers meetings could be held unmolested. Agreement was reached at the meeting comprising of representatives of the Citizen Army and the trade union movement on the following points: '1) The Irish Citizen Army would be extended beyond the Dublin area and the force would be known as the Irish Workers Army. 2) That initially as an act of good faith a certain amount of money would be given to provide for the immediate purchase of certain small arms. The Union premises at 17 High Street were to be placed at the disposal of the Irish Citizen Army. 3) Further meetings were to take place in pursuance of future development' (Robbins: P. 233). Unfortunately these ideas remained exactly that, ideas, and came to nothing. However had these basic plans come to fruition the bombing of the Four Courts and the seizure of important documents by the enemy may not have been so damaging to the organisation whose membership would have covered a greater expanse of terrain instead of been confined to the Dublin area.

When the order came from Frank Aiken, 24th May 1923, to all Anti-Treaty troops in the field to dump arms and Cease-Fire it signalled the end of the Civil War. For the Irish Citizen Army this marked the beginning of the years of semi-obscurity, though this did not mean at that time the Citizen Army ceased to exist. However it did mark the beginning of the end for any input they may have had on the Irish political landscape. The next major public display by the Irish Citizen Army, as was mentioned, was not until 1927 the sad occasion being the funeral of Constance Markievicz.

During the mid 1930s a new left wing organisation came into being, the short lived Republican Congress. The Republican Congress, 1934-36, was an organisation which advocated a Workers Republic and proclaimed itself, at its launch on 8th April 1934, 'so revolutionary that its achievement means the overthrow of all existing political and economic machinery which at present holds this country and our people in subjection. Therefore our call is: Workers and working farmers unite to the Workers Republic' (*The IRA*: Tim Pat Coogan: P. 78). Amongst the most notable of Congress recruits were Nora Connolly O'Brien, the daughter of James Connolly, and her brother Roddy. With the rise of Fascism across Europe during the 1930s, most notably Bennito Mussolini in Italy and Adolf Hitler with his misleadingly named National Socialism in Germany, the Republican Congress called for a united front against this ideology in Ireland fronted by Eoin O'Duffy and his Blue shirts (also known as the National Guard, League of Youth, Army Veterans and other guises). In its newspaper, *Republican Congress*, it called for a united front against Fascism and for the Workers Republic. Differences were, however, building up within the ranks of the Republican Congress and these came to a head at a convention held in Rathmines Town Hall on 29th and 30th September 1934. A comrade named 'Michael Price differed from the majority of delegates on methodology and consequently was not elected to the executive. Price wanted the organisation to concentrate on strikes, resisting eviction, and the creation of a political organisation to contest municipal and Dail elections' (Coogan: P.79). Others including George Gilmore did not consider it the right time for such a programme, and first wished to establish cells within the trade union movement and placing their men in key positions within existing political organisations. At this point Price and his followers took the decision to leave the Republican Congress and joined the remnants of the Irish Citizen Army, which although ageing and smaller in size was still in existence. This move by Price from the Republican Congress to the Citizen Army stands as evidence that the organisation was still in existence eleven years or so after the Civil War came to an end. Peter Berresford Ellis's earlier contention that the Civil War signalled the end of the Citizen Army can be questioned by this fact. It would be true enough to concede that the last political shots fired in anger by members of the Citizen Army was in the Civil War but it would be premature to assume that this period signalled their final demise. The irony is that at the point of Price's departure Nora Connolly O'Brien and her brother were harbouring ideas to transform the Republican Congress into a new, younger, Citizen Army perhaps within the existing structures of the present organisation or if necessary with modifications to meet the changing times.

In 1947 the first Commandant the Irish Citizen Army ever had and founder of the Irish Transport and General Workers Union, Jim Larkin, died. This was perhaps to be the last public parade by the army now consisting of ageing men and women who, despite their years, were as proud then as they were thirty four years previous when the army was first addressed by the man in the coffin. 'There were crowds at Jim Larkin's funeral- just as there were crowds in Jim Larkin's life. A half of century of history marched through Dublin yesterday morning. The years were crowded between Haddington Road and Glasnevin. You couldn't think of Larkin being in that flowered covered coffin with its Starry Plough flag, just dead'.

'They all came out, men in dungarees with overcoats buttoned up to the throat, marching erectly as he told them to march. It could have been a Citizen-Army-cum-Volunteer parade, only for the slowness. The very air of the city seemed to be muffled. You had the feeling that the people were magnetised into the funeral as by common instinct.

And the men in dungarees and the women grown old who have borne children since they struck instinctively at the 400 bosses at Larkin's will, seemed to be there just because they had to be there' (*The Lion of the Fold*: Donal Nevin et al. P. 353).

The men and women of the Irish Citizen Army were as proud in their latter years as they were in their prime and they did their former Commandant proud. As Liam Mac Gabhann describes the scene 'groups that line the sidewalks, waiting, saying nothing, move out, walk after the old grey men of the Citizen Army, after the tired women of the hopeful eyes of the Citizen Army' (ibid).

This was perhaps the last parade of the Irish Citizen Army and I dare say an emotional one at that. As the 1940s moved into the 1950s the ageing men and women of the Citizen Army became more of an old comrades club, for the want of a better description. Veterans of the 1913 Lockout and the Easter Rising along with the Anglo Irish War and the tragic Civil War would meet occasionally over a few pints of stout reminiscing the proud days of their history. Under later legislation former members of the Citizen Army would receive a pension and a medal in respect of National Service subsequent to 1916 and prior to 11th July 1921 (see Appendix 5). Many of the statements used during the compilation of this work were written in the early to mid 1950s and extracts from these have been used courtesy of the National Archives, Dublin.

In 1937 Eamon De-Valera took practical advantage of the situation which arose following the abdication of Britain's King Edward Vlll. With Britain without a monarch it would be possible to hold a referendum on a new constitution, as was permissible under British law under the Statute of Westminster 1931. The constitution was republican in all but name and the position of Governor General was to be replaced by that of a President. The 1937 constitution claimed sovereignty over the whole thirty-two counties of Ireland even though the Dail could still only legislate for twenty-six of them, and the new name of the country was *Eire*. In 1949 the coalition government under the leadership of John A. Costello declared the twenty-six counties of Ireland a Republic while still claiming sovereignty over the whole of the Ireland. This was again amended as part of the Good Friday Agreement, amending articles 2 and 3 of the constitution. Neither the 1937 constitution nor the declaration of a republic in 1949 would live up to the criteria set by James Connolly and the Citizen Army for a workers republic.

The 1937 constitution and the declaration of a republic in 1949 did not really cause the British Government any real concerns. The feeling in London was something along the lines of, so the Irish no longer consider themselves part of the British Commonwealth, and claim sovereignty over "Northern Ireland", so what!. It was of little consequence to the British side it was, after all, only words which were never taken seriously by the Crown. Unlike the Anglo Irish war where words were backed up by actions thus forcing some limited negotiations on the subject of Irish independence the latest grand sounding echoes reverberating around Dublin were simply words of hot air which to the British were not worth the trouble of re-occupation or any other form of action. As for Irelands claim of sovereignty over "Northern Ireland" which was never, and still is not, recognised under international law (if such a concept exists) and for them, the Irish, the conventional military option was a non starter so what was the worry. The Irish bourgeoisie were quite happy to pay lip service to this claim thus giving the rest of the population something to think about other than poverty and their British counterparts were happy enough to allow this illusion to continue, providing that is all it remained, an illusion.

Perhaps had the Costello administration started doing something politically radical, to give their claim of a republic some teeth, along socialist lines previously advocated by Larkin, Connolly and the Citizen Army this would almost certainly have caused the British concern. We should remember Connolly's statement: "If you remove the English army tomorrow and hoist the green flag over Dublin Castle, unless you set about the organisation of the socialist republic, your efforts would be in vain", well the English army have been removed and not much had/has changed for the working class. Instead they paid, and still do, mere lip service to Connolly, his ideas along with those of 1916, and make no effort what so ever to implement them. If the 1949 declaration had declared Ireland a "Socialist Republic" with a programme of nationalisation for all financial institutions and industry, with a view to the common ownership of the means of production distribution and exchange under workers control, production for the need of the population instead of the profits of a few fat cats, then this would have presented a completely different scenario. Such a scenario which the Atlee labour Government in London, despite nationalising around five percent of their own industry, could not ignore. They would have kept a close eye on, to say the least, the socialistic activities of the Irish. If, as part of these radical changes (remember we are talking about an alternative political system of governance), the Twenty Six county administration had began restructuring the "Defence Forces" along the lines of the Irish Citizen Army constitution and thus swearing to uphold those five principles, the 1949 declaration would have contained some teeth. Teeth capable of bringing about real social change, equality and working with organised labour towards these ends. If, for example, this new Citizen Army had been ordered to seize the means of production control and exchange for, and as part of, the working class with the establishment of workers soviets (councils) as a means of administering industry democratically, then we would almost certainly have seen a reaction from the British bourgeoisie and their Irish allies. This hypothetical reaction, by the British bourgeoisie, would have been still born if the proletariat (working class) of Britain had been moving in tandem with those progressive forces in Ireland and forced the Atlee Government into implementing the complete socialisation of society, including the public ownership of the means of production distribution and exchange. Under such conditions the problem of partition would not have existed as socialism as an ideology is based on mutual co-operation and the sovereignty claimed under the 1949 declaration would have become a reality, as opposed to no longer swearing an allegiance to a foreign Monarch (some may ask what all the trouble was about). A genuine socialist administration in London would have handed back the Six Counties as part of Irish national territory to the socialist Irish Government. Back to reality and these things unfortunately did not happen, the "Defence Forces" do not subscribe to the constitution of the Irish Citizen Army, the means of production are not publicly owned and the banks are not nationalized. Basically Ireland is a mirror image of what it was under British rule with a few alterations to create an impression of independence, not the same as full true liberation.

One thing is perhaps certain and that is if in 1949 a socialist republic had been declared there would have been a violent response by both the British and their counter revolutionary allies in Ireland. Among these forces we can number the church, higher echelons of the "Defence Forces", the Gardai and of course the private owners of the means of production. The same reaction would, in all probability, occur today if there was to be, either through popular revolution or plebiscite, a Marxist administration installed in Ireland along with all the trappings like the Citizen Army as defenders of the new socialist system. Put simply the freedom of any country does not exist if the majority of that country are chained by the shackles of capitalism. Irish, and countries like her, bourgeois freedom is only permitted providing their political structures run in tandem with those of the bigger capitalist countries. Any country which enslaves another can never itself be free, which is why the peoples of the USA, Britain and countless others, if they could only see it, will always be slaves of the same class of people who enslave other countries like Ireland. As it stands Britain would never allow a socialist Ireland, the British state will not even allow a socialist government in Britain let alone in her "own back yard". To add to this dilemma we also have the European Union to contend with and this organisational group of countries insistence on all its member states promoting the concept of "free competition". European Union member states can not, under EU law, implement any policies which interfere with the idea of "fair competition". Even Keynesian economics is all but illegal! In electoral terms this amounts to the electorate of any member state not being allowed to vote into office a socialist government. They can certainly elect a party which may call itself Socialist, but, should this newly elected governing party of any given member state try to implement socialist policies they would encounter huge problems simply because these policies would be an antithesis to "fair competition" and therefore the European Union..

It would not be compete to end this brief *Descriptive History of the Irish Citizen Army* without asking the question, is there a modern equivalent of the Irish Citizen Army? Indeed is there a need for one? I shall try to examine these thoughts in a short epilogue after a brief summary.

* * *

17

Summary

When speaking of the Irish Citizen Army it is very important to speak of it within the political environment which it grew up in. While it is perfectly true that both Jim Larkin and James Connolly were avid internationalists, orating international solidarity, it must be remembered that at the same time there were members of the army who were nationalists though, it must be added not in the same way as far right groups of more modern times speak of "nationalism", or "national chauvinism", but in the context of "national liberation" which, it should be equally remembered is also a component of internationalism in its socialist sense. Given the fact that the ranks of the Irish Citizen Army was filled with activists from organised labour the army was always going to have the edge of radicalism over the Volunteers.

At the time, unlike today, coming from the socialist camp the only internationalists were indeed socialists. It was only necessary for any socialist of the day to use the word "socialist" for any listener who understood anything about the subject to gather the speakers views were "internationalist". This was why, perhaps, it was not paramount for the volunteers of the Citizen Army, remembering its birth was before the Russian Revolution, to over emphasise "internationalism". Today however with capitalism taking on a more global nature, both in theory and reality, the word "internationalist" is no longer necessarily specific to socialism. It is, therefore important today to stress "international socialist" and not merely "internationalist".

The Irish Citizen Army was formed as a workers defence force in November 1913. It was modelled, ironically, on the Ulster Volunteer Force created by Edward Carson in 1912. Addressing the Dockers and Carters at a meeting in Berresford Place Jim Larkin advised the men to "take Carsons advice to the men of Ulster". "If Sir Edward can call on the people of Ulster to arm, I will call upon you to arm. If they have the right to arm, the working men have an equal right to arm so as to protect themselves. If at every street corner there is a hired assassin ready to kill you then you then should arm". The concept of a Citizen Army was first introduced at a meeting of the Industrial Peace Committee, early in November 1913, which had been formed by Professor Tom Kettle MP and which also included writers and other prominent citizens. It was proposed at this meeting by Captain Jack White that an army be formed to bring discipline to the ranks of the locked out men. The proposal at this meeting was ruled out of order but at a later meeting, held in the rooms of the Rev. R.M. Gwynn at Trinity college, on 12th November 1913 the idea was suggested again and this time accepted. The notion of a Citizen Army was met with great enthusiasm from James Connolly, then deputising for the imprisoned Jim Larkin, at Liberty Hall. So the die was cast for the development of the first revolutionary red army in Western Europe of the 20th century. The question is was the idea of a Citizen Army unique?, or was it a copy of Carsons invention in Ulster? Or more diversely did it have echoes of the events which took place in Paris in 1870-71 or Moscow in 1905? Certainly if the idea was the work of the second meeting of Industrial Peace Committee in the rooms of Rev Gwynn then it could be certainly considered unique. On the other hand if this was only a suggestion and it was, in fact, Jim Larkin who ran with it and turned the suggestion into an idea then it could well have a certain carsonite odour about it, however for far different reasons which must be remembered. Finally if it was James Connolly who took the suggestion and moulded it into a notion there could well be traits of the Paris Commune or the 1905 insurrection in Moscow interwoven.

Whatever the fundamental roots of the Irish Citizen Army were it quickly became the military arm of organised labour in Dublin. Starting from a position of defending trade union activists, strikers, supporters and their tenement communities during the 1913-14 class conflict in Dublin the Irish Citizen Army graduated into the custodians charged with the defence of Liberty Hall and all inside it. The Citizen Army was also to the fore in the defence of the ITGWU bandsmen and their equipment as well as helping prevent evictions of unemployed and striking workers. When the 1916 Proclamation was being printed inside Liberty Hall it was the Irish Citizen Army to whom the protection of the printing equipment and the printers themselves was entrusted under the command of Lieutenant William Partridge. The personnel of the Citizen Army very soon, through necessity, gravitated into arms manufacturers. Part of Liberty Hall was transformed into an armoury for this purpose. Although the army had weapons for around two hundred there is little doubt that had the equipment been available they could have paraded ten times that number.

In line with socialist policy and practise the Irish Citizen Army advocated and practised gender equality within its ranks. It may have been found wanting in this department only on the grounds that it perhaps did not give the women the full recognition they deserved. If this was the case it was almost certainly unintentional. We must also remember that the period we are talking of was the early part of the 20th century, a time when women's equality was very much in its infancy, a time when the suffragettes were still struggling for the vote. Apart from the Women's Suffrage organisations it is difficult, outside the labour movement, to find any group which gave even lip service to the emancipation of women. The Irish Citizen Army were certainly pioneers of this ideology in Ireland.

The men and women of the Citizen Army were among the first to go into action during Easter Week in the City hall vicinity and were the first to suffer a fatality in the form of

Captain Sean Connolly. At the St. Stephens Green Garrison it was the Irish Citizen Army, under the command of Michael Mallin and Constance Markievicz, who came up with the idea of continuing the war in the hills when the surrender order was received. The volunteers of the Citizen Army refused to surrender until they had clarification that the order came from James Connolly, their own Commandant, who had indeed countersigned the document. The signature of Padraic Pearse alone on the surrender order would have been insufficient for the volunteers of the Citizen Army to surrender themselves and their weapons.

The flag adopted was the Plough and the Stars, otherwise referred to as the Starry Plough, of which there appears to be some confusion over its origins. The flag was, according to Frank Robbins of the Irish Citizen Army, designed by a Mr Megahy. However Sean O'Casey, Hon. Secretary to the army in the early days, in a letter to Jack Carney gives us a different picture as to the origins of the flag. 'Jim [Larkin] tells me he designed the flag of the Plough & the Stars. Fox in his book quoted the *Irish Worker* (April 1914) as saying it was the work of Mr Megahy; AE told me HE done it; and I, who was Secretary [of the ICA] then, don't know who done it (sic). I'm inclined to think Jims fancy thought of a design like it...; that AE was asked to draw it and paint it, that Megahy was asked to do it, then. Anyway he knocked out a design (I have it here), but it was just a plough shape sprinkled with stars, cruedly representational. Finally, if I remember right, Dun Emer did the flag and gave it a stylistic touch which really made it very beautiful. It was the finest flag - in design and execution - Ireland had ever had' (extract from Sean O'Caseys letter to Jack Carney: *James Connolly A Full Life* Donal Nevin: P.555). There also appears to be some confusion as to the colour of the background of the original Starry Plough flag. It has been reported by some quarters that the background was green, a description I have always accepted, however Sean O'Casey in 1954 'presented the original design of the flag referred to in his letter to Carney to the National Museum,

O'Casey pointed out that the flag was oblong, much longer in its length than its width, bordered by red - brown tracing with a frill fringe of deep and dark yellow, probably meant to be orange. The field was blue' (Nevin P.556). The men and women of the Irish Citizen Army were disappointed that the field in the design was blue and not green, and it is believed that this disappointment was the leading factor which led to the change from blue to green when the flag was made. This is an important point to remember that we are talking about the design and not the finished product. Despite the apparent confusion as to who designed and made the flag one irrefutable fact remains and that is: during the Easter Rising it was the Starry Plough, the flag of the Irish Citizen Army and Irish Labour, which flew over the citadel of Murphy's capitalism, the Imperial Hotel, on the orders of James Connolly.

The Irish Citizen Army were the first to go into action during Easter week 1916. They were in action in and around the City Hall and Dublin Castle under the command of Captain Sean Connolly who became one of the first, if not the first, combatant casualty of the rebellion. In hindsight they, the Citizen Army, should perhaps have taken Dublin Castle given the numerical weakness of its defenders however this was not known at the time. Shortly after the events taking place around Dublin Castle and the City Hall the Irish Citizen Army were in action at St. Stephens Green under the stewardship of Michael Mallin, Connolly's second in overall command, and Constance Markievicz who in turn was Mallin's immediate deputy. Once again with the gift of hindsight perhaps the decision not to take the Shelbourne Hotel, due to a perceived shortage of personnel, was an error of judgement which cost the garrison dearly during the events of the following days.

Throughout the rising the Irish Citizen Army maintained its autonomy from the Irish Volunteers despite James Connolly's public oration stating that "there no longer existed a Citizen Army and a Volunteer force. There was now only the Irish

Republican Army". This was of course at odds with Connolly's earlier statement to the men and women of the Irish Citizen Army regarding the holding on to weaponry "as those with whom we are fighting may stop before our goal is reached. We are out for economic as well as political liberty". Further evidence of the autonomy possessed by the Citizen Army can be found in the evidence given by Police Constable 212C John O'Connell, Dublin Metropolitan Police, at the Court-Martial of Michael Mallin. He stated 'The Citizen Army and the Irish Volunteers are two distinct bodies. The Citizen Army is under the control of James Connolly. There is a slight difference in the uniform of the two armies' (Barton 277).

After the rising captured volunteers of the Irish Citizen Army along with the Irish Volunteers were herded off to various prisons and camps across Britain and Ireland. As the reader will recall Frank Robbins account regarding the attitude held by some elements within the population of Dublin when the POWs were being marched to Richmond Barracks. It will be recalled that groups of pro-British elements were shouting slogans in support of the Staffordshire Regiment and were even shouting for the British soldiers to shoot the rebels. In other parts of Dublin the captured insurgents were subjected to having rotten fruit and eggs thrown at them along with other obnoxious projectiles. I wish it could be said with confidence that if a similar situation arose today the same mentality would not prevail unfortunately I am not wholly convinced.

Only when the British establishment, represented by the personification of General Sir John Maxwell, began the executions of the leading insurgents and some rebels who did not hold leadership positions, meaning signatories of the Proclamation, did public opinion begin to swing from one of hostility to sympathy favouring the revolutionaries. The actions of these people towards the very same who were fighting for their, the peoples, freedom could be described as something akin to the scene in Robert Tressell's (real name Robert

Noonan) novel *The Ragged Trousered Philanthropists*. In this scene the socialists were attacked by a baying mob of working class men, the very dispossessed people which socialism was trying to liberate from the chains of bondage they awoke to every day, it was these same would be liberated people in the scene who actually wanted to kill the would be liberators. The difference been this description was a fictional scene, though no doubt very much in line with the thinking, or lack of it, within the lower echelons of society at the time in a novel, whereas what happened in Dublin is historically factual. The change in public attitudes was to manifest itself a couple of years later in the 1918 General Election which resulted in a massive vote in favour of republican candidates (though I must repeat the idea mooted by Lord French to introduce conscription earlier in the year also contributed). The point of concern is that at the end of the rising it took the execution of fifteen men (sixteen if we include Sir Roger Casement hanged in London) for a change of opinion within the general population in support of the rebels.

There would appear to be some confusion or conflicting interpretations as to what Jim Larkin's opinion of the Easter Rising was and, more to the point what he thought of the Citizen Army being involved at all. According to the historian Peter Berrsford Ellis 'Larkin expressed his disappointment that he had not been in Ireland to take part in the rising: Though fate denied some of us the opportunity of striking a blow for human freedom, we live in hope that we, too, will be given the opportunity'(Berresford Ellis: P.235). This would suggest that Jim Larkin was in favour without reservations of the rising however Irish Citizen Army volunteer Frank Robbins gives a different account. He suggested that when he met Larkin a year or so after the rising in the United States he, Larkin, denounced the rising as a purely nationalist venture. He condemned Connolly for taking part in the exercise and particularly for leading the forces of organised labour, "it should have been left to the poets", the Irish Citizen Army down this path. On this subject it must be remembered that Peter Berresford Ellis, reliable as he is, was drawing on second hand information in formatting his conclusion to Jim Larkins attitude towards Easter week. Frank Robbins on the other hand was reciting a personal meeting with Larkin and by virtue of this fact this is the more likely version of events regarding the position of the former chief.

After the rising many Irish Citizen Army personnel were imprisoned in various camps around Britain. Shortly after his release Frank Robbins sailed for the United States where the above meeting with Jim Larkin took place. On his return the Citizen Army was barely recognizable to the army which took part in the rising. Some of the new personnel were not wholly trusted due to past issues. They had a new Commandant, James O'Neil, who turned out to be less than up to the job. When the Anglo Irish war, 1919-21, began the Irish Citizen Army took no part as an organisation but many individuals and groups certainly did much against O'Neil's wishes. They kept their individual identities as Citizen Army people despite coming under the overall command of the IRA. Citizen Army personnel took part, during this war, in exercises such as intelligence, espionage, and arms procurement all of which were vital tasks in the prosecution of the war. Some were attached to the Dublin Brigades intelligence unit where top secret full time work was undertaken. When the IRA undertook a daring day light attack on the Customs House the Irish Citizen Army volunteers were gutted that they, as an army, were not involved. This caused much resentment against O'Neil, resentment which the reader will recall was well founded.

During the Civil War which ensued following the signing of the treaty, Decmber 6th 1921, many Citizen Army volunteers refused to take either side, or, in other words, take up arms against fellow Irishmen. Others, on the other hand, decided, all be it with some reluctance, to take the anti-treaty side against the fledgling Free State and its British supplied army. Once again the Citizen Army per se took no part and those who did came under the command of the IRA once again maintaining a certain amount of identity autonomy. The historian Peter Berresford Ellis contends that with the *Free State* bombing of the Four Courts, where most of those Citizen Army volunteers involved in the Civil War were positioned, and the subsequent capturing of documents during this bombing that this was the final demise of the Irish Citizen Army. However further investigation based on historical facts would suggest that this was not the case. It may be perfectly true to argue that the army never fired another shot in anger they did maintain their structure and discipline and therefore existence for many more years to come.

When the Civil War came to an end in 1923 it would be reasonable to say that a period of low revolutionary activity, to say the least, was conspicuous by its absence throughout the country. The Irish Citizen Army though still maintaining its structures was more or less inactive. The next time the organisation would publicly appear was to be the funeral of Constance Markievicz in 1927. At the funeral the Irish Citizen Army led the procession of mourners which also included the new Fianna Fail party of which Constance was a founder member along with Eamonn De Valera in 1926. In modern times this may sound ironic, an army of such revolutionary tradition on the same march of respect as a party which was to eventually become as equally reactionary as Cumann na nGaedhael (Fine Gael) once it gained political power. It may also sound ironic that a person of Constance's political ideology and beliefs should have anything to do with Fianna Fail given the pro capitalist stance it was to take however we must remember that everything is all well and good with the gift of hindsight.

The Citizen Army Guard of Honour at the funeral of Constance Markievicz was a credit to all those men and women who made up its formation. However once this sad event was concluded the role of the Irish Citizen Army once again sank into obscurity with lack of clarity, on this Peter Berresford Ellis is correct. As the 1920s moved into the 1930s the Citizen Army, still technically in existence as no formal disbanding had taken place, was becoming more of a memory to all but those still politically active than a living reality. However in 1934 the skeleton staff within the remnants of the army became involved in a new left republican organisation the Republican Congress. On April 8th in Athlone a conference voted to form this new revolutionary venture. Notable members of the congress with Citizen Army connections and membership were Nora Connolly O'Brien, who was a signatory at the Athlone conference, and her brother Roddy Connolly, both the children of James Connolly. Nora was at one time a messenger for the Irish Citizen Army and the ITGWU. The congress had its own newspaper the *Republican Congress* which was its main organ of communication. The support for the congress came mainly from the workers and small farmers and one of its major functions and objectives was working for a united front against the rising tide of fascism and the march towards a Workers Republic. The Republican Congress, despite the Trojan efforts of such people as George Gillmore, Frank Ryan, Roddy Connolly and Cora Hughes, was short lived and by November 1936 this brave left wing initiative which perhaps offered the last lifeline of activity for the remains of the Citizen Army ceased to exist.

With the fall of the Republican Congress and, in 1938, the ending of the economic war with Britain the remaining members of the Irish Citizen Army could do little more than maintain contact with each other and continue to work for the interests of the working class through the labour and trade union movement and perhaps the Communist Party of Ireland. When the Spanish Civil War broke out in 1936 some Citizen Army veterans, although strictly speaking were getting past combat age, volunteered to fight for the Spanish Republic against the reactionary fascist forces led by General Franco.

The next and final time members of the Citizen Army would be seen as and marching as a body would be the sad passing of big Jim Larkin in 1947. The funeral though, like that of Constance

Markievicz, sad was very well attended as men and women from across Dublin took to the streets. The now ageing men and women of the Irish Citizen Army formed a guard of honour and no doubt looked as smart and proud as they did on April 24th 1916 when in, arguably, their finest hour they marched from Liberty Hall in formation to take up positions around the city to take on an empire.

With the funeral and burial of Jim larkin over the Irish Citizen Army itself would begin to die of natural causes. Some of the younger volunteers like Frank Robbins would live for another few decades and he even wrote a book the contents of which have contributed greatly to this work. Through the 1950s the elderly men and women of the Irish Citizen Army would meet and reminisce regularly, just like old soldiers of any army would do, and no doubt there was no shortage of material for discussion. One can only envy any fly on the wall at any of these veterans get togethers.

**

18

CONCLUSION

Since the idea for the formation of an Irish Citizen Army was first floated in those tea rooms at Trinity college the development of the army in such a short period of time was really quite a remarkable achievement in itself. Through its various stages of development from workers defence force to an instrument of revolution in less than three years there was one ingredient perhaps, with the gift of hindsight missing. The missing piece of the jigsaw to complete the picture was perhaps the absence of a revolutionary socialist party. Such a party could have given the army direction in the political field and such a party could also have kept the Irish Citizen Army a place on the playing field after 1916 and the death of Connolly and Mallin. Even though James Connolly was instrumental in the formation of the Irish Labour Party this organisation never became the political voice of the Citizen Army. On the contrary as the years passed it rapidly became, like its British counterpart, a party of reform and not revolution and in the much celebrated 1918 general election even stood aside to give Sinn Fein a clear run. This was perhaps a mistake the labour movement would never recover from.

The failure to form a revolutionary Marxist party was perhaps, with hindsight, a mistake. Once the army was committed to the path of revolution the presence of a political party and voice became increasingly more important. As we have noted the military defeat of Easter week and the execution of Connolly and Mallin did not signal the end of the Irish Citizen Army. With the rise of James O'Neill whose knowledge of socialism would appear to have been akin to that of a donkey on the beach the army lunged from unwittingly being a tool of O'Neill's to biting at the bit for an organisational part in the war of independence. O'Neill, as history has recorded was all about what was good for him with no regard for the socialist cause at all or that of the working class in general. A revolutionary socialist party linked closely with the Irish Citizen Army could have given direction in the second reorganisation of the army after 1916. Such action as the formation of a party may well have avoided the catastrophic events which occurred at leadership level within the army.

Any organisation whose aim it is to alter the political system or landscape must have a collective view of politics. This means having a political organisation operating alongside, though non combatant role, and not separately from the revolutionary army. The same political party could , under certain circumstances, use the ballot box as a tool to measure its level of support for the idea of socialism and true democracy but only for this aim. To use the bourgeois ballot box as a means of taking part in their game of exploitation is a betrayal, unless to expose their institutions for all to see. Had this happened who knows in the 1918 general election the political arm of the Irish Citizen Army could have performed well. This, however, we will never know.

The same political party personnel would be also active, as were many Citizen Army members, within the trade unions and in the workplace at the point of production. The party and army personnel would work in tandem as part of the same movement. If there had been a political party in existence there appears to have been little reason why certain members with an aptitude for both political and military affairs could not have held dual membership of the Citizen Army and the revolutionary party. However this position does have its potential problems and one is if an activist is holding dual membership which hat and when is that person wearing. I would argue the party should always take the political decisions, which would include the direction of the army, but this is obviously easier said than done. So despite little reason existing as to why it could not happen there would still be problems which would have to be ironed out. However on a similar note we should remember that the womb of the Irish Citizen Army was the Irish Transport and General Workers

Union and dual membership was held there with no problems! They were part and parcel of the same movement, a movement which could have consisted of the ITGWU, Irish Citizen Army and a revolutionary socialist party (as this did not happen a party name is not essential). The need for a political party is only one avenue of socialist revolution and not necessarily the only route.

Perhaps a major factor contributing to the lack of a political party, and this is presented purely as a possibility, was that essentially both Jim Larkin and James Connolly had sympathies with a revolutionary trait known as syndicalism. Syndicalism is a version of trade unionism which peaked in the years preceding the First World War, though strands of this ideology still prevail in certain quarters to this day. Syndicalism seeks control of society by direct strike action leading to co-operative workers control of industry. Strikes, and especially the strategy of the general strike which is seen as the weapon to bring down the capitalist mode of production and with it the entire bourgeois system. Syndicalism perceives these methods as the only legitimate and useful tactics for organised labour to take in pursuit of socialism. There are two important consequences of trade unions accepting a syndicalism position, one being tactical and the other theoretical. The former impact, and if the theory is correct the one which may have had an impact on Larkin and Connolly's thinking, is the refusal to make political alliances with socialist parties. A political party and particularly a parliamentary one was seen as revisionism. The second consequence, more theoretical, was to force a breach with orthodox communist parties, because the syndicalist insistence on workers control and ownership of the means of production clashed with the theory of democratic centralism. If this theory holds any water it is more likely to have been the former, rather than the latter, factor which may have influenced the thinking of Larkin and Connolly. Perhaps then, as today, the would be revolutionary parties of the socialist left were incapable of agreeing with one another which paints Syndicalism as an alternative option.

However if this theory is correct, and it is only a theory, it would appear that in the case of James Connolly it may not have always been the case, after all did he not form the Irish Socialist Republican Party in 1896?. Perhaps James Connolly's experiences in the United States and his involvement with the Industrial Workers of the World (Wobblies) a revolutionary syndicalist trade union may have had some influence on his thinking. It should also be remembered that the same James Connolly was instrumental in the formation of the Irish Labour Party (which bears little resemblance to today's version of the same name) so as can be seen there are holes in the theory. That concluded it must be added that the Irish Labour Party was never aligned to the Irish Citizen Army and the ISRP predated it. It is my belief that Connolly's experiences with syndicalism in the USA did have a lasting affect on his political thinking particularly after his fall out with Daniel De Leon and, as was Larkin, perhaps a supporter of syndicalism all along which may well have been a leading factor in the absence of a political party aligned to the Citizen Army. Perhaps the political party strategy was always a second option towards the same goal of socialism for James Connolly. Syndicalism is, in my opinion, the ultimate revolutionary goal where a party is at the end of the day unnecessary and workers elected and accountable deputies form the governing body. That said to go from A to Z of the alphabet there are another twenty four letters to go through. It could be argued that a revolutionary political party is a necessary evil to guide the revolution towards the correct Marxist conclusion. The same party should be prepared to disband itself once the overthrow of capitalism has been achieved. This disbandment should be staggered as more power goes to the workers councils. Once again theory.

As has been pointed out James Connolly was instrumental in the formation of the Irish Labour Party. One issue which promptly persuaded Connolly of the need for an independent labour party in Ireland was the subject of partition. In 1914 the British Labour Party ignored resolutions from the Irish Trade Union Congress, instead adopting resolutions from the constitutional Irish Party. When the Irish representatives from

the ITUC proposed the formation of an independent Irish Labour
Party the British Labour Party refused. The Irish congress in
1914 urged the British Labour Party to oppose the partition
of Ireland and, if necessary, to vote against the entire Home
Rule Bill in order to prevent it. Once again the British Labour
Party followed the lead of the Irish bourgeoisie, through the
Irish Party, in supporting partition. This was an important issue
for James Connolly who had worked tirelessly against partition
and constantly warned against any form of it from the first day
the idea was floated. This was a leading factor, among others,
in his thinking around the formation of the Irish Labour Party.
However the fact that James Connolly was a founder member
of the Irish Labour Party and at the same time was active in
the Irish Citizen Army should not lead to the wrong conclusion
that the two were fused. It must not be seen in the same light
as the relationship between the Irish Citizen Army and the Irish
Transport and General Workers Union.

James Connolly was a committed Marxist Revolutionary who
explored many avenues towards the ultimate goal of socialism.
He followed the route of party aligned with class, tested the
water of party politics and took a well documented interest in
syndicalism. During Easter Week he also took the nationalist
path this, however, should not be mistaken with the chauvinistic
nationalism which later was to give rise to fascism. Connolly's
nationalist approach was, or should have been more appropriately
called, the national liberation theory and was certainly, as some
historians have tried with little success to suggest, not a break
from socialism. It would be a big mistake to consider Connolly's
decision, through consultation with the army rank and file, to
take the Irish Citizen Army into the Easter Rising as a break
with the ultimate objective of a workers republic.

Jim Larkin, the first secretary of the Irish Transport and
General Workers Union and Commandant of the Citizen Army,
perhaps initially had stronger leanings towards syndicalism
than did James Connolly. It is unlikely that Larkin would have

been diametrically opposed in theory to the revolutionary party but perhaps did not see this a point of primacy. Syndicalism does not see the need primarily for a party as the ideology of ONE BIG UNION (OBU) is the vehicle to drive the proletariat towards the ultimate goal of socialism. There are arguments for the existence of a political party, arguments which still go on today, and reasons against.

The syndicalism theory being the leading factor as to why there was no revolutionary party attached to the Irish Citizen Army is only one, and others may differ in their views. It could also have been felt, if the subject was ever discussed, that a political party may have its own agenda to follow which could have been at the expense of the army. Either way there is one undeniable fact and that is that the first two commandants of the Irish Citizen Army, Jim Larkin and James Connolly, both had to a greater and lesser extent strong leanings towards the model of syndicalism.

When Jim Larkin left Ireland for the shores of the United States of America James Connolly assumed command of the Irish Citizen Army and took up the role of acting secretary of the ITGWU. From this point the army was to enter its revolutionary stage whose ultimate aim was to force a British withdrawal from Irish shores and the establishment of a socialist republic with the means of production under workers control. As always the central question of which most others spring from on this subject, then as now, is who owns the means of production, distribution and exchange? A question seldom asked within the ranks of the Volunteers but which was central to Citizen Army doctrine. However this move into revolutionary mode did not distract the Irish Citizen Army from its initial role as a workers defence force, on the contrary it complemented this role. Connolly firmly believed only the power of the working class could ever free Ireland in its true sense. Freedom does not mean the removal of a foreign occupier and usurper to replace them with an indigenous variant of exploiters who consider themselves and themselves alone as the nation, with the majority working class there to "serve the nation". This is not freedom it is merely painting the room a different colour with the room essentially remaining the same. In order to truly free Ireland, or any other land, the working class must free itself from the chains which bind it and in the process free Ireland. The capitalist class are interested only in profits and new markets to amass even higher gains through the exploitation of labour. This could/ can be achieved either under an administration of occupation or an independent Irish government on behalf of the native bourgeoisie, as we are seeing today. However at the time the Irish bourgeoisie needed to be free of British interference and so equally did the proletariat of Ireland. Easter week could in one respect epitomise the class collaboration of the time, though Connolly was under no long term illusions. The chief aim of the Irish capitalist class in an independent Ireland was one of freedom to exploit the indigenous working class and exploit new markets without any, or minimal, interference from the imperial power in London. The working class, Connolly argued, by freeing itself from the British yolk would also march forward to free itself from indigenous Irish capitalism. To this end Connolly could see no contradiction in using the Irish Citizen Army as an instrument of revolution even if the insurrection was essentially of a nationalist variant. After a successful revolution it would be the working class which would constitute the nation and not the minority capitalist gang. National Liberation would be a more appropriate term to describe the Citizen Army position and should not be confused with chauvinistic, ethnocentric nationalism.

With or without a political party it is undeniable that the Irish Citizen Army was the first armed workers militia of Western Europe in the twentieth century. It is important to stress Western Europe because, arguably, the events of 1905 in Moscow, which is Eastern Europe, could equally be argued was the theatre where the first Red Army in the whole of Europe had the stage. It is almost certain that had Connolly known of the events which would occur in Russia a year later in 1917, the Russian Revolution (October 25th by the old style Julian calendar, November 7th by the more modern Gregorian calendar), he may well have held off and waited for that moment. How great we all are with the gift of hindsight. The Irish Citizen Army first used as a defence force of the locked out workers during those hard and bitter months of 1913/14 developed into an armed force capable of challenging the planets largest empire. Whether a revolutionary political party would have given the Citizen Army a broader and deeper perspective thus enabling it to enter the theatre of political life, making the whole movement three pointed consisting of the Irish Transport and General Workers Union, the Irish Citizen Army and a political wing using the weapon of politics and military action with greater success we shall never know. If we look at the recent developments within Sinn Fein (Provisional) and the IRA we **may** see possibilities of what **might** have happened. If such a scenario had occurred, and my belief is that it may have been beneficial with limitations, the party should have at no point entered elections with a view of reforming capitalism. Elections could have been used as a barometer to measure the level of support among the population for revolutionary socialist ideology. It could also have been used as a platform aimed at getting the message of exploitation across to the masses and formatting revolt thus breaking the chains of bondage. However as this did not happen it tends to sink into the realms of what might have been and that we will never know for certain.

One undeniable factor since the formation of the Irish Free State in 1922, declared a republic in 1949, is that not one government has taken any of James Connolly's politics on board. Despite much of the 1916 Proclamation having many echoes of the constitution of the Irish Citizen Army this has been conveniently ignored. There is nothing today to suggest anything different is on the horizon.

EPILOGUE

Is There A Modern Equivalent Of The ICA?
Is There A Need For One?

It is true enough to say that times have moved on since the days of the Irish Citizen Army but has the passage of time fundamentally changed anything within the mechanisms of the society which dictates our lives? The structure of society, i.e. that based on class, or the haves and have not's, the private ownership of the means of production still remains. The powers that be have learned the lessons, to a certain extent, from the past and, it is true to say, in most Western liberal democracies including Ireland people do not starve. However the contradictions within the structures of a capitalist society are as inherent today as they were in the days of Connolly and the height of the Citizen Army. What is the major defining factor which shapes the society we live in? With a little thought and examination it will be seen that this defining factor is the same now as it was in the days of Larkin, Connolly and the Citizen Army. The question, which all others stem from, is who owns the means of production, distribution and exchange and the answer is the same now as it was then, the bourgeoisie or capitalist class in other words private ownership as opposed to that of public ownership and workers control. It is true to say that the passage of time and, therefore, development within the capitalist system has changed the face of this class, for example today capitalism is a collection of global phenomena as opposed to the domestic variant which predated this spread. Today we have transatlantic corporations and multinational companies owned by a few groups of private capitalists whom the working class are still at the mercy of. Unemployment can strike any individual or family at virtually any given moment as many of these large companies move to other countries to expand their markets and where the wages paid are lower. Either workers, in Ireland or anywhere else, work for lower wages thus undercutting each other or these firms will find less well off people who will.

At the same time as the face of the capitalist class has changed so too has that of the working class, the proletariat, particularly with the fall in heavy industry to be replaced by the service, finance and managerial sectors along with lighter forms of industrial production. What should also be taken into account, along with the aforementioned changes in the style of employment is the increased number of employees occupied in the Information Technology (I.T) sector, not only in Ireland but around the globe. This represents another major change in the mode of daily work.

Despite this changing face it does not detract from the fact that they, the working class, still sell their labour power for a monetary wage thus making them the "working class" of post modernity. The means of production themselves are more advanced than ever, which is not a problem in itself, with computers and computerised machinery replacing the older types of equipment. The problem is, now as then, who owns and benefits from these technological advancements? For the working class it inevitably leads, in many cases, to unemployment and a lower standard of living, for the bourgeoisie it is normally the reverse, leading to greater prosperity. Such innovations as team work, small teams of workers with a team leader, have replaced many of the older fordist (so called after the motor car manufacturer Henry Ford) conveyor belt methods of assembly, and team leaders have supplanted the supervisor, charge hand and foreman system of control. Small industrial units have replaced many of the old style factories and other forms of heavier industries. Office blocks are springing up all over the place as the finance sector grows, and so the changes are endless. The one factor which, however, has not changed is, not to sound too repetitive, who owns all the new technology and computerised inventions? Answer the same class of people who owned the means of production a century ago, the capitalist class who, then as now, accumulate huge profits out of the labour power of others.

On the issue of national liberation not a great deal has changed in this department either. The British Crown still control the six counties, albeit militarily on behalf of NATO (North Atlantic Treaty Organisation) to a large though not exclusive extent, just as they did when the treaty was signed back in 1921, and arguably the United States have a military presence in the South due to their use of Shannon Airport. Arguably, because the armed forces of the USA have reportedly shown their presence outside, well outside, the confines of the airport. In fact reports in various media outlets in 2006 claim they have been sighted as far away as County Clare in uniform! Much of the twenty six county economy is controlled by the actions of companies from other countries, notably the United States. These companies employ Irish workers and many of the goods and services are for the Irish market, they are calculated into Irelands Gross Domestic Produce (GDP) however the profits of these firms are enjoyed by shareholders in the USA, as part of the US Gross National Produce (GNP), and not Ireland. Such rights as those afforded under article 40 of the Irish Constitution stating "the right of citizens to form associations and unions" are ignored by many multinational companies, in much the same way as W.M. Murphy did in 1913.

The issue stemming from this brief description of modern industrial relations is, is there a modern equivalent of the Irish Citizen Army? Secondly do we need one? I shall try to answer the second part first. If we go back to the class conflict of 1913 one of the fundamental issues at stake between W.M. Murphy and the Employers Federation, and Jim Larkin and the ITGWU, was the right of workers to join a union of their own choosing. Murphy said no, Larkin said yes. Murphy refused to recognise the ITGWU or allow any of his employees to join without facing dismissal. When the employees stood firm he, and other employers, locked them out of their employment stating that they could return to work only when they gave a written undertaking disowning the ITGWU. This gave rise to the class conflict which followed and the birth of the Irish Citizen Army to counter police brutality.

It could be argued that much the same is happening today, even though it is unconstitutional, with many transatlantic companies refusing to recognise any trade union. As for police brutality advocates of the present system would argue that the modern Irish police force, An Garda Siochana, do not brutally beat pickets to the ground. To this it should be countered that only so long as the pickets are obedient and do not represent a threat to the status quo or have any notions about changing society in their own favour does police aggression not occur. They are allowed to picket providing the only threat they pose is by walking round in circles like headless chickens. If these pickets were to do anything more menacing such as occupying the premises of the firms they are in dispute with, organising mass and flying pickets or taking sympathetic action, a favourite of Jim Larkin's, we would see a much more aggressive attitude from the Gardai on behalf of the state, in much the same way as the police force in Britain battered striking coal miners to the ground during the 1984/85 miners strike. This is of course more liberty than workers could expect in police or fascist states and it would be misleading to refer to Ireland as being such a state yet.

As we have witnessed at demonstrations, as opposed to picket lines, Gardai have on occasions become very truncheon happy and hydro active with the use of water cannon. In November 2007 Gardai acted in, according to television footage, in a very heavy handed manner outside the Corrib gas refinery site at Rosport, Co. Mayo. The protesters at the time were part of a campaign against the multinational company Shell, a campaign which became known as "Shell to Sea". One protester described the Gardai as a "private police force for Shell". The Gardai, on the other hand, defended their actions blaming the protesters for any disturbance. However judging from the television footage it certainly looked as though the protesters had more than a valid point. The outstanding question could cynically be asked, would An Garda Siochana have behaved in such an aggressive manner had a Citizen Army or modern equivalent been present? From this point of view a modern equivalent of the Irish Citizen Army could be deemed necessary. On the other hand if we take the pluralist position on industrial relations, that "class conflict is inevitable but not insurmountable", or in simple terms trade disputes can be resolved without violence through the machinery of collective bargaining, that is if firms recognise trade unions for this purpose which increasingly more do not. If this machinery can provide all the cures for the ills of the working class then we quite evidently do not need a Citizen Army. So the question could be put another way, can capital and labour co-exist indefinitely? As was discussed above the answer is probably not!

The present economic system which we are forced to live under is known as capitalism. Its continued existence is dependent on the triumph of capital over labour, put bluntly the employers maintaining their rule over the employees with a few minor concessions here and there to maintain a visage of fair play. The political system which governs this class ridden society is liberal democracy, liberal by way of the rights of the individual, usually the employers, over the common interest of the majority. The rights of private property over public or common ownership are enshrined in this system. The democracy part of this imbalance occurs every four or five years when elections come around and we are asked to vote for the party considered best equipped to conduct the affairs of capitalism. To the vast majority of voters, the working class, very little changes particularly in property relations and the relationship to the means of production for them. The uneven weighting of liberalism over democracy could be summed up thus LIBERAL democracy, democracy for five minuets at election times. As the one time British labour Lord Mayor of London, Ken Livingstone, once said "if voting changed anything they would abolish it". Under this system we are all, in theory, equal before the law. Once again this can be questioned under careful examination. There have been cases on several occasions, a case at Black Rock Dublin in 2006 springs to mind, involving people from the families of big business resulting in the loss of life, in other words murder. The sentences meted out by the courts have been substantially lower than corresponding cases for people from working class backgrounds though both are equally wrong. Persons who hold public office who are given jail sentences are usually given shorter terms of imprisonment, and more privileges, than people of less prominence.

Capitalism is about the bosses squeezing as much productivity out of the workers as possible and giving as little in return as they can practically get away with. Thus maximising profits which are why firms are in business to start with, the provision of goods and services are secondary.

Some firms, to be fair, are more considerate towards their workers than are others but those who concede too much to their employees go out of business. The reverse side of the coin is that it is in the interests of the labour force to get as much out of the employers as possible, thus increasing their living standards, for shorter hours and lower production in certain circumstances to prevent overproduction resulting in redundancy. This is the inherent contradiction within the capitalist system, the maximisation of profits against increased real wages and better working conditions, shorter hours etc. These contradictions lead to an unstable system in which peoples jobs are not secure and the weaker companies go out of existence again resulting in job losses. Any group, or groups, of workers and small business people who fight against this anarchy will meet the full power of the state. If a government were to be elected, even under these rules, which advocated the nationalisation of the larger companies, including the United States transatlantic corporations they would meet stern opposition. How long would the United States Army stay within the confines of Shannon

Airport before they intervened to take back the companies for their former owners and exploiters? How long would the British stay North of Dundalk if such a nationalisation policy was introduced in the twenty six counties? The Irish state would be well aware of the potential eventualities and to prevent such scenarios occurring would ensure that radical government, elected or otherwise, would never reach fruition. Once again the employers, despite numerical inferiority, have the advantage with the state and foreign allies behind them along with their ability to transfer capital at will. The proletariat, on the other hand, with numerical superiority have very little apart from the mechanics of collective bargaining and many, who work for companies which do not recognise trade unions, don't even have that. Looking at the situation from this angle a variant of the Irish Citizen Army looks essential, however this depends on a persons political point of view normally dictated by their position in society.

Now let us briefly examine the second part of the question, "is there a modern equivalent of the Irish Citizen Army"? It is firstly important to take a brief look at the possible candidates starting with the Official Republican Movement, arguably the parent body of modern republicanism. Their political voice is the Workers Party, formerly Sinn Fein the Workers Party, and their military arm is the Official IRA, a term afforded them by the media in the early days to differentiate between themselves and the more aggressive Provisionals. The Official IRA has been on ceasefire since 1972 and from that time has had very little impact on the national liberation question. However the Workers Party have been involved in such class based issues as fighting evictions and trying to achieve their political pivot of uniting Protestant and Catholic workers, a laudable position but not as easy as it sounds certainly in the North of Ireland. There are those who argue that too much emphasis has been placed on this issue to the negation of the national question.

Then we have the Provisional Republican Movement (the name Provisional was dropped by the movement in 1990 but has resurfaced again in recent years). Their armed wing, or perhaps former armed wing due to their act of decommissioning, is the Provisional IRA and its political voice is Provisional Sinn Fein, ever growing in support since the ceasefire of PIRA in 1996. The Provisional IRA waged a long guerrilla war against the British forces and establishment in the North of Ireland which some critics argue was to the detriment of the class conflict. The Provisionals split from the Officials in 1969-70 due to the latters reluctance to supply arms for their Northern units to use in the defence of the nationalist areas against loyalist mobs who were carrying out ethnic cleansing at the time. The Provisional IRA proved themselves worthy defenders of the nationalist communities and perhaps their most notable, and first defence, was that of St. Mathews churchyard, Short strand East Belfast. This is a small nationalist enclave of around six thousand inhabitants surrounded by sixty thousand loyalists. The Officials reportedly concerned themselves little with these defences because, it is claimed, shooting at loyalists, belligerents or otherwise, would be an antithesis of their policy which was aiming to unite Protestant and Catholic workers.

At the 1986 Provisional Sinn Fein Ard Fheis (National Conference) a motion was tabled which aimed to drop the party's policy of abstaining from Dail Eireann. Abstention was, and is, felt by republican traditionalists as a fundamental principle of the word. It was also one of the reasons for the Provisional's split with what became known as the Officials. At the Ard Fheis, January 1970, the then unified Sinn Fein passed a motion allowing the party to, in the new conditions prevailing at the time, enter the Dublin parliament, Dail Eireann. This, claimed the group about to become the Provisionals, was against the principles of the Second Dail 1921 and all that Irish Republicanism stood for. Now history was about to repeat itself, not for the first time, and produce a split from the Provisionals for the same reason. When a motion to drop the policy of abstaining from the Dail was tabled and carried, a group under the leadership of Ruairi O'Bradaigh and the late Daithi O'Connell, and had amongst their number one of the last surviving members of the Second Dail, Commandant Tom Maguire, left the conference to form a new party, Republican Sinn Fein which was to later develop its military wing, the Continuity IRA. One of the major policies of Republican Sinn Fein is a federal system within a United Ireland, Eire Nua (New Ireland) which envisages a provincial parliament for each one of the four provinces and a federal parliament for the whole country. The leadership of Republican Sinn Fein were the former hierarchy of Provisional Sinn Fein, and at the time they too adopted Eire Nua as policy, before the Northern leadership assumed control referring to Eire Nua as "a sop to Loyalism". Republican Sinn Fein are not generally known for their involvement in the politics of class conflict perhaps, from their point of view, seeing such issues as a distraction from partition, similar to the Volunteers claiming back in 1913 "there was no room for local disputes this is national business" to the Citizen Army. The Continuity IRA have carried out armed attacks on the British forces and unlike the Provisionals are not presently on ceasefire.

In April 1998 Provisional Sinn Fein signed up to the now famous Good Friday Agreement (sometimes referred to the Belfast Agreement or the Stormont Agreement or Accord). In order to be allowed into the multiparty talks on this agreement all those who were considered to have a military wing had to ensure that part of their organisation was on ceasefire. The Provisional IRA met this criteria and as a result Sinn Fein were eventually allowed to enter the talks on devolved government for "Northern Ireland". The Provisional IRA have, what is termed under the Good Friday Agreement, reportedly decommissioned their weapons and as a result Sinn Fein are in devolved government, as the largest nationalist party, with the Democratic Unionist Party at Stormont. They also have at present 14 Tds in the Dail. However the leadership of the movement do often speak of their policy regarding "workers rights" particularly in their European context. It should be remembered that, despite the positive tones of this ideology, that workers rights within the capitalist system are not the same as workers control of the means of production, distribution and exchange. They have moved away from any involvement in conflict politics, class conflict leading to a change in the balance of class forces or other forms of conflict, and could perhaps be described as a radical left wing constitutional party, some would even question this description. The membership of the Provisional Movement is what could be described as a broad church covering the whole political spectrum. The left wing are still involved with the trade union movement though this progressive side is counterbalanced by a powerful right wing element some of whom see no contradictions between the interests of business and those of the workers. Out of this complete change of political direction by the Provisionals another split occurred. A small group styling itself the Real IRA emerged, and gained (rightly or wrongly) infamy for the bomb which went off in Omagh claiming 31 lives in August 1998. The Real IRA do have a political voice, though not a party as such, the 32 County Sovereignty Committee. Once again the issue of class struggle is not this organisations priority.

Another small group to emerge from the shift in the provisional movements policies and may lay claim to historical kinship with the Irish Citizen Army are a Socialist Republican organisation called Eirigi. They like many others fly the Starry Plough and lay claim to the Socialist Republican tradition which many of their day to day activity would certainly enhance. This group like most others are often seen on demonstrations in support of striking workers along with a united Ireland and are as entitled as any other organisation to lay their claim with more justification than most.

The final contestant, if that is the correct term, on the list of possible candidates to claim the mantle as the ideological inheritors of the Irish Citizen Army, comes the Irish Republican

Socialist Movement consisting of the Irish Republican Socialist party, the Irish National Liberation Army and the Republican Socialist Youth Movement. It is the second component which is of primary concern to our purpose. The movement was formed in 1974 by a number of republicans, trade Unionists, socialists and other progressive leftwards thinkers under the stewardship of Seamus Costello after a split with the official republican movement. The main aims of the organisation was/is to unite the national and class struggles under the one umbrella with the slogan "for national liberation and socialism" in much the same way as James Connolly fused the two issues into an inseparable single. Seamus Costello and many others since him, like Thomas "Ta" Power and Gino Gallagher could see that it is impossible to have true national liberation without the emancipation of the working class. All three of these working class revolutionaries were assassinated on 5th Oct. 1977, 20th Jan.1987 and 30th Jan. 1996 respectively.

The IRSM claims to be a revolutionary Marxist organisation and basis much of its ideology on the teachings of James Connolly and their interpretation of his variant of Marxism. The organisations members and supporters march behind a red banner depicting the embroidered heads of Karl Marx, Frederick Engels, V.I. Lenin and James Connolly and the movements colour party parade the Irish National flag, the Starry Plough, the flags of the four provinces and, perhaps most notably, the Red Flag. More historical similarities between the IRSM, and particularly the INLA, and the Citizen Army can be found on page 11 of the organisations Easter 2007 issue of the *Starry Plough* which states . '*He led a small armed force, the Irish Citizen Army, who ideologically were the predecessors of the INLA, with no ideological difference what-so-ever, against the British Government, and it was against the will of the majority of the time. The majority did not support the Rebellion and, in fact, some even fought against it. It's just like today and it's all down to ignorance coupled with the effectiveness of Imperialist/Capitalist propaganda. In 1916 they used violence, they used guns and explosives but it was to achieve a politically sound objective. This was the terrorism through the eyes of the state, again, just like today'* (authors italics). As can be gleaned from the tone of this statement the claim is that there are ideological similarities linking, historically, the Irish Citizen Army, particularly in Connolly's time, and the INLA of today.

The INLA have been involved in many guerrilla actions against the British establishment and perhaps the most notable was the attack, which resulted in the death of Margaret Thatcher's friend and right hand man Airey Neave. This attack took place in the British House of Commons car park in 1979 and came as a severe blow to the future British Prime Minister, Margaret Thatcher of who Neave was a close political confide. Like the Provisional IRA the INLA are presently on a recognised ceasefire though the IRSP are not signatories to the Good Friday Agreement. The IRSP have been involved in many campaigns in defence of working class interests such as anti-drugs work, trade disputes, anti-racist activity and promoting the defence of nationalist working class communities in the North. They have also had involvement in international campaigns for example Hands off Cuba and Venezuelan solidarity campaigns. Their political ideology, it is claimed, is based on an alteration in the balance of class forces thus placing the working class at the hub and in control of the means of production, distribution and exchange.

It is stated unambiguously in a document written by Thomas Power entitled the *Ta Power Document* : 'We must make no secret of the fact that we are a revolutionary socialist party, prepared to give leadership on the streets as well as in the elected chambers, and that we are out for a socialist republic (or a revolutionary socialist state) part of that struggle for a socialist republic entails resolving the national liberation struggle and ending British imperialist intervention'. Can we hear echoes of James Connolly and not mere lip service from this movement?.

To conclude it must be said that under the present conditions it is virtually impossible to have a mirror image of the Irish Citizen Army. The freedom of publicly drilling and bearing arms afforded to the Citizen Army and the Irish Volunteers would never be peacefully tolerated by either the Irish authorities in the twenty six counties or the British in the six. It may be perfectly true to say that, as is referred to in the IRSM Easter 2007 magazine, the Irish Citizen Army are the **ideologica**l predecessors of the INLA and, judging by what written evidence of this exists, there can be little doubt of this historical connection. However can anybody imagine either the British or Irish states allowing, for the sake of historical sentimentality, INLA personnel to parade publicly and bearing arms anymore than the variants of the IRA could imitate, what some would argue to be their ideological forebears, the Irish Volunteers to openly parade in the same fashion? Such a scenario under the present status quo would be unlikely to say the least. To answer the question is there a modern equivalent to the Irish Citizen Army perhaps the question should be is there a modern IDEOLOGICAL equivalent, there we may have an answer. Certainly on the written evidence mentioned the INLA could appear to be the only organisation laying claim to this inheritance, though it must be remembered this is a claim. Some may ask why no loyalist organisation has been mentioned as candidates for a modern equivalent to the Citizen Army. The answer should be obvious. The Irish Citizen Army were out for a free Socialist Workers Republic in Ireland with no capitalist or imperialist interference. A complete breaking of the British connection. Loyalists on the other hand are out to maintain partition, which the Citizen Army were opposed to, and the British connection. One is an antithesis to the other. It must be remebered though that the loyalist UVF (Ulster Volunteer Force) take their historical tradition from a certain Edward Carson and if we recall

Jim Larkin "if its good for Carson and the men of Ulster its good for the working men of Dublin"!

Is there a need for a modern equivalent of the Irish Citizen Army? To answer this, or attempt to, we should examine the behaviour of the liberal democratic states, not just in Ireland but in other countries also. Take France where we have often seen demonstrators and trade unionists battered to the ground by truncheon happy gendarme (French Police) and saturated by water cannon. In Britain surely many can remember the scenes of striking coal miners being brutalised by the police during the 1984-85 strike for simply trying to defend their jobs and communities. Here in Ireland we have witnessed Gardai using water cannon and batons on Mayday demonstrators resulting in the hospitalisation of demonstrators and Gardai in the dock before a judge. Each individual must make up their own mind on this question, and, in many cases what conclusion they arrive at will be determined by preconceived ideas and class prejudices.

If there is a need for a modern variant of the Irish Citizen Army there are many changes and changing circumstances which must be taken into account. Firstly when the original organisation was formed back in 1913 it was primarily for the fight against a native capitalist, William Martin Murphy, who, although ruthless only operated at the time within the shores of Ireland (though many of his ideas were exported) primarily, if not exclusively in Dublin. To strengthen his position he cemented a coalition of like minded employers and went on to form the "Employers Federation" which consisted of four hundred of his disciples. The trade union, ITGWU, responded in kind by seeking the assistance of other trade unions, around 37 of them, some of whom had members locked out of their employment for showing sympathy towards the Transport Union and its members. Jim Larkin and the ITGWU also sought the intervention of the British Trades Union Congress, who were frankly of little help, and also appealed to the trade union rank and file in Britain who, unlike many of their leaders, were great allies. The employers upped the stakes further by involving the "Shipping Federation" which employed non-union labour who were prepared to scab. The Citizen Army, at this stage, was still in its picket defence force stage and fought back against police brutality and also defended its own band players and property. The important factor to look at is Murphy's involvement of the "Shipping Federation".

We should now take a leap forward in time of ninety five years or more. In these days of post-modernity capitalism is very much a global concept. Not only have the employers joined forces in defence of their own interests across Dublin they have done so across the planet. This fact, if ever a modern equivalent of the Irish Citizen Army were to be recognised should not be minimised. If it was ever felt among the radical circles of working class organisation that a Citizen Army, or equivalent of, was needed it is, in all likelihood, almost certain that it would have to fight employers from more than one country, the multi-national companies. This being the case the multi-national could, and in all probability would, shift operations to another country of operation, therefore it is likely that the forces of organised labour would also have to be operational in other countries outside of Ireland. Such an organisation could not, therefore, be reasonably called the "Irish Citizen Army", perhaps the Workers International Defence Force would be a more appropriate name. For example a fight for union recognition against one of thee large corporations based in Ireland could spread to one or more of that companies operations in France, Germany or any other country where they operate, an injury to one is an injury to all. Therefore it would follow that the tentacles of any modern workers defence force, based on the initial reasons for the formation of the Irish Citizen Army, would have to reach these countries which would be no easy task particularly with international capitalism arming itself to the teeth. The Irish wing of such a movement would still have to combat the existence of partition, this should not be neglected.

Secondly and of equal importance on the home front organised labour faces problems which it did not necessarily have to confront in the days of Jim Larkin and James Connolly. It is perfectly true that today we have the successor to the "Employers Federation", IBEC, to confront along with right wing indigenous governments but we also have the curse of racism, which as suggested earlier it can only be concluded Connolly would be to the fore fighting against, within the workplace which the employers use, sometimes subtly other times more overtly, to create artificial divisions among the workers. It may well be necessary for any modern organisation wishing to claim the mantle of the Irish Citizen Army to confront not only IBEC and other employers organisations on the industrial front but also their allies, in some cases, of the far right on the political stage. This, unfortunately, is the modern theatre where today's industrial and class confrontations are enacted and racism is only one tentacle of the problem of artificial divisions among the proletariat. Racism was also around, though to a slightly lesser extent in James Connolly's day, most commonly in the form of anti-Semitism in common with centuries of anti Jewish persecution, often leading to pogroms against this section of society. In the 1902 Wood Quay local election the ISRP, with Connolly as their candidate, contested on the socialist ticket. Connolly aware of the Jewish working class community and eager to make the elections all inclusive issued, from the Fishamble Street offices of the United Labourers Union, election statements in Yiddish calling on the Jewish workers to vote for the Socialist candidate. This all inclusive method was not dissimilar to that of the Independent Workers Union in modern Ireland who have their literature printed in Chinese, Polish and other minority languages to reflect the needs of the modern proletariat. James Connolly was certainly ahead of his time back in 1902 and the writing of literature in Yiddish was specific to the ISRP. Therefore, just as the future Commandant of the original Irish Citizen Army viewed with panoramic perception that even at that time there were ethnic minorities within the working class who needed to be addressed it would naturally follow that any modern equivalent of the army would have to reflect the multi-cultural, ethnic and racially diverse working class which is a progressive feature of modern Ireland in much the same way the original organisation would have done. Evidence, as earlier discussed, of this assumption could be seen in the gender equality policy adopted by the army of the day combating sexist stereotypes which existed at the time which Connolly in particular spearheaded. Another example of Connolly's commitment to racial equality occurred during his tour of the USA in 1902. Shortly after his arrival in New York Connolly visited Newburgh in New Jersey the house which was George Washington's headquarters during the revolutionary war of independence. On the wall of this house was something which he, Connolly, found paradoxical. The offending memorabilia was the will of George Washington's mother. Among the contents of her will were a few lines where she bequeathed to one of her children , 'my Negro wench, little bit, and all her future increase' This Connolly found totally contradictory and he commented "here we have the family of the greatest patriot of Revolutionary America- a patriot passionate with love of freedom - consigning to perpetual servitude, not only the living Negro woman, but all her children yet unborn. It forms another illustration of the necessity for insisting upon a clear definition of the term freedom as of all other terms so glibly used in political warfare".

These two examples should help the reader, if any help is needed, to answer any questions of where Connolly would have stood in today's modern multi cultural and diverse society in Ireland. James Connolly is perhaps the most broadly known of all the Commandants of the Irish Citizen Army and his ideologies and politics of achievement perhaps epitomised the army as a whole.

Therefore possibly in the context of today's society perhaps just "Citizen Army", as many of today's working class culturally identify themselves as much with their countries and ethnic origins as they do with a sense of being Irish, could be a more reflective title. Who's to say with any sure confidence?

When the original Irish Citizen Army was formed at the meeting held in the rooms of the Rev. R.M. Gwynn at 40 Trinity College on November 12th 1913 it must have appeared a mountainous task which, for the time, it unquestionably was. However in today's world, and for the reasons briefly outlined above, among many others, that mountain would appear more like a sand dune, which does not mean to say that given the prevailing circumstances at any given time the project should not go ahead. The necessity for a modern variant of the Irish Citizen Army can not be decided on these few pages, as we would move too far away from the title of the work, but in the event of circumstances deaming such a formation necessary all aspects must be taken into account.

The Irish Citizen Army was, as we have discussed, the armed revolutionary wing of organised labour. It was a component factor in the struggle for socialism of which national liberation from a foreign power was an integral aspect. Arguably the army's most notable commandant, James Connolly, was not only struggling for socialism but in the long term was using the method of syndicalism to that aim. This ideology based on the theory that no political party is ultimately necessary is one which he attached himself to during his days in the USA and involvement with the Industrial Workers of the World. Due to the fact that the struggle for socialism in Ireland, national liberation included, has not yet been achieved the ideology behind the Irish Citizen Army and its formation it would theoretically follow must be relevant today. The offending system of capitalism based on the principle of exploitation is as entrenched as it ever was. This fact tends to make the idea of organised labour having a military wing tangible in theory if not for the moment pragmatic.

In today's society of uncertainty leading to capitalist instability regarding workers employment it is often disheartening for activists and those fighting for socialism and, therefore a fairer society, to see elements within the ranks of those who would actively benefit from such a society, the working class, showing open hostility to socialist ideology. However like most coins there are two sides and the other side of the negative, and the one which activists must always look to, is the positive. Organised labour through the centuries has proved that it will fight back if pushed by the exploiters too far. It is on this positive note that I must disagree with Francis Fukuyama who suggests that the ideology of socialism/communism based on Marxist theory is dead.'The passing of Marxism-Leninism first from China and then from the Soviet Union will mean its death as a living ideology of world historical significance' (Modernity And Its Futures; edited by Stuart Hall, David Held and Tony McGrew: P. 48). This assertion that socialism is dead is simply not true. Francis Fucuyama uses countries which arguably never were socialist, in its true sense, as examples to support his wishful thinking. If socialism as an ideology is dead why then are there in various countries active and vibrant shop stewards movements, rank and file workers organisations and revolutionary socialist, Marxist, movements across the globe? Like most ideologies socialism, as does the tide, ebbs and flows. It may be true that at the moment we are ebbing but as sure as night follows day after every ebb there is a flow. What the capitalist system should beware of is that this flow does not become an unstoppable tidal wave taking all before it, including their profits.

As for modern inheritors of the Irish Citizen Army the reader must decide for themselves whether any of the above mentioned organisations come up to the mark and qualify for this inheritance.

Appendix 1

Manifesto Sent To Irish Trades Bodies
Irish Citizen Army Headquarters,
Liberty Hall, Dublin

The Secretary.............................. Trade Union
A Chara----In view of the present situation it has been decided to reorganise and develop the scope of the Irish Citizen Army. No one knows what a day may bring forth. We have Ulster Volunteers preparing for eventualities in the North, and National Volunteers actively organising themselves in various parts of Ireland, while all the time the Labour Hercules leans foolishly on his club.

Would it not be a shame if the forces of labour alone were content to believe all things, suffer all things, endure all things,; to starve rather than take, to be stricken and not strike back?

Believing that labour will shake itself into action, we have formed a provisional council to develop the power and influence of the Citizen Army in labour circles, and we hope their efforts will receive the co-operation of your Trades Union. We promise to hold a meeting in your........................... Shortly, and in the meantime, we appeal to you to use your efforts to prevent the members of your union from joining organisations, however attractive its name or principles may seem, till we have the opportunity of fully explaining to them the principles, objectives and aims of the Irish Citizen Army.

We enclose copies of constitution, posters and handbills, and hope that these will show that the Irish Citizen Army is the only suitable organisation for the workers of Ireland.
Fraternally yours President, Captain White, DSO,
Hon. Secretary, Sean O'Cathasaigh
Irish Citizen Army

Appendix 2

First Handbill Issued To Irish Citizen Army

Why Irish Workers Should Not Join The Volunteers

1) Because many members of the Executive are hostile to the workers.
2) Because it is controlled by the forces that have always opposed labour.
3) Because many of its officials have locked out their workers for asserting their right to join a trade union of their choice.
4) Because they refuse to definitely declare that they stand for the democratic principles of Wolfe Tonne and John Mitchel.
5) Because they welcome into their organisation creatures that are proved renegades to their own class.

Reasons Why Irish Workers Should Join The Irish Citizen Army

1) Because it is controlled by leaders of your own class.
2) Because it stands for labour and the principles of Wolfe Tonne, John Mitchel and Finton Lalor.
3) Because it has the sympathy and support of the Dublin Trades Council.
4)Because it refuses to allow into its ranks those who have proved untrue to labour.

Workers Don't Be Misled; Trust Only Those Who Ye Know And Have Suffered For Your Class.

Join The Irish Citizen Army Now!

APPENDIX 3

(Front Page)

The Irish Citizen Army
Membership Card
1913

President
Captain White Dso

Hon Secretary
Sean O'cathasaigh

Hon Treasurers
Countess Markievicz
Richard Brannigan

Army Headquarters
Liberty Hall Dublin

GO go uiridh Dia an Rath Orainn

(Back Page)
"The land and sea and air of Ireland for the people of Ireland. That is the gospel the heavens and earth are proclaiming, and that is the gospel every Irish heart is secretly burning to embrace" *John Mitchel*

APPENDIX 4

The Constitution Of The Irish Citizen Army

1) That the first and last principle of the Irish Citizen Army is the avowal that the ownership of Ireland, moral and material, is vested of right in the people of Ireland.

2) That its principle objects are:-
    A): To arm and train all Irishmen capable of bearing arms to enforce and defend its first principle.
    B) To sink all differences of birth, privilege and creed under the common name of Irish People.

3) That the Irish Citizen Army shall stand for the absolute unity of Irish Nationhood and recognition of the rights and liberties of the worlds democracies.

4) That the Citizen Army shall be open to all who are prepared to accept the principles of equal rights and opportunities for the people of Ireland and to work in harmony with organised labour towards that end.

5) Every enrolled member must be, if possible, a member of a Trades Union recognised by the Irish Trades Union Congress.

God Save The People

Appendix 5

'Summary of views on the disbursement of the funds of the Sinn Fein organisation. For example, the finance officer in the Department of Defence refers to a scheme drawn up in 1936 for the establishment of the National Veterans Benevolent Fund. This scheme provided for assistance of destitute members, and their families of a number of organisations including the Irish Citizen Army'.

'21st March 1942 Memorandum to the Government from the Department of Defence, 21st March 1942, relating to the issue of a medal in respect of National Service subsequent to 1916 and prior to 11th July 1921. The Minister proposes that two medals should be struck, a 1916 medal and a general service medal. All persons have been awarded service under the Military Service Pensions act and those who did not apply for a pension, but who satisfy the Minister that they rendered service between 1916 and 1921 will be issued with a medal. A deputation of the Old IRA and kindred bodies met the Taoiseach and the Minister of Defence and put forward certain proposals. For example they proposed, that the interpretation of Active Service be of a wider nature than that given under the Military Service Pensions board for the purpose of distribution of the medal'. (Source: National Archives, Citizen Army cabinet files, Department of the Taoiseach: Military Service file 1916-21, Issue of General Service Medal).

Appendix 6

Names Of Those Executed By The Crown After The 1916 Rising.

The seven signatories of the proclamation will appear first.

Padraic Pearse	Irish Volunteers
Thomas MacDonagh	Irish Volunteers
Thomas Clarke	Irish Volunteers
Eamonn Ceannt	Irish Volunteers
Joseph Plunket	Irish Volunteers
James Connolly	Irish Citizen Army
Sean MacDermott	Irish Volunteers
Edward Daly	Irish Volunteers
William Pearse	Irish Volunteers
Michael O'Hanrahan	Irish Volunteers
Sean MacBride	Irish Volunteers
Sean Heuston	Irish Volunteers
Con Colbert	Irish Volunteers

Thomas Kent   Irish Volunteers
(Cork Detention Barracks)

Michael Mallin   Irish Citizen Army

Roger Casement   Irish Volunteers
(Hanged in London)

BIBLIOGRAPHY

A History Of Irish Flags by G.A. Hayes-Mcoy

The Lion Of The Fold by Donal Nevin Et Al

The History Of The Irish Citizen Army by R.M. Fox

The Story Of The Irish Citizen Army by P. O'cathasaigh

The Rebel Countess by Anne Marreco

The Life And Times Of James Connolly by C. Desmond Greaves

From Behind A Closed Door by Brian Barton

The History Of The Irish Working Class by P. Berresford Ellis

Under The Starry Plough by Frank Robbins

The Irish Civil War 1922-23 by Eoin Neeson

James Connolly's Selected Writings by P. Berresford Ellis

James Connolly's Selected Works. .Volume 2

The Plough Easter 2007 / Irsp Publications

The Ta Power Document / Irsp Publications

The Ira by Tim Pat Coogan

Ireland Her Own by T.A. Jackson

James Connolly A Full Life by Donal Nevin

In The Footsteps Of Big Jim (A Family Biography)
by Jim Larkin Jnr.

Newspapers Dunlaoighre Express 9. 11, 07

Modernity And Its Futures Edited By Stuart Hall, David Held
And Tony Mcgrew.